Black Religion / Womanist Thought / Social Justice
Series Editors Dwight N. Hopkins and Linda E. Thomas
Published by Palgrave Macmillan

"How Long this Road": Race, Religion, and the Legacy of C. Eric Lincoln
Edited by Alton B. Pollard, III and Love Henry Whelchel, Jr.

African American Humanist Principles: Living and Thinking Like the Children of Nimrod
By Anthony B. Pinn

White Theology: Outing Supremacy in Modernity
By James W. Perkinson

The Myth of Ham in Nineteenth-Century American Christianity: Race, Heathens, and the People of God
By Sylvester Johnson

Loving the Body: Black Religious Studies and the Erotic
Edited by Anthony B. Pinn and Dwight N. Hopkins

Transformative Pastoral Leadership in the Black Church
By Jeffery L. Tribble, Sr.

Shamanism, Racism, and Hip Hop Culture: Essays on White Supremacy and Black Subversion
By James W. Perkinson

Women, Ethics, and Inequality in U.S. Healthcare: "To Count Among the Living"
By Aana Marie Vigen

Black Theology in Transatlantic Dialogue: Inside Looking Out, Outside Looking In
By Anthony G. Reddie

Womanist Ethics and the Cultural Production of Evil
By Emilie M. Townes

Whiteness and Morality: Pursuing Racial Justice through Reparations and Sovereignty
By Jennifer Harvey

Black Theology and Pedagogy
By Noel Leo Erskine

The Theology of Martin Luther King, Jr. and Desmond Mpilo Tutu
By Johnny B. Hill

Conceptions of God, Freedom, and Ethics in African American and Jewish Theology
By Kurt Buhring

The Origins of Black Humanism in America: Reverend Ethelred Brown and the Unitarian Church
By Juan M. Floyd-Thomas

Gifts of Virtue, Alice Walker, and Womanist Ethics

Melanie L. Harris

palgrave
macmillan

First published in 2010 by
PALGRAVE MACMILLAN®
in the United States—a division of St. Martin's Press LLC,
175 Fifth Avenue, New York, NY 10010.

Where this book is distributed in the UK, Europe and the rest of the world,
this is by Palgrave Macmillan, a division of Macmillan Publishers Limited,
registered in England, company number 785998, of Houndmills,
Basingstoke, Hampshire RG21 6XS.

Palgrave Macmillan is the global academic imprint of the above companies
and has companies and representatives throughout the world.

Palgrave® and Macmillan® are registered trademarks in the United States,
the United Kingdom, Europe and other countries.

ISBN: 978–0–230–61511–3

Library of Congress Cataloging-in-Publication Data

Harris, Melanie L., 1975–
    Gifts of virtue, Alice Walker, and womanist ethics / Melanie L. Harris.
        p. cm.—(Black religion/womanist thought/social justice)
        ISBN 978–0–230–61511–3 (hardback)
        1. Walker, Alice, 1944— —Criticism and interpretation. 2. Walker,
    Alice, 1944— —Ethics. 3. Walker, Alice, 1944— —Religion. 4. Spirituality in
    literature. 5. Virtues in literature. 6. Values in literature. I. Title.

PS3573.A425Z67 2010
813'.54—dc22   2010014003

A catalogue record of the book is available from the British Library.

Design by Newgen Imaging Systems (P) Ltd., Chennai, India.

First edition: October 2010

10 9 8 7 6 5 4 3 2 1

Printed in the United States of America.

To Survivors
May we all be truly free and live our beauty in wholeness.

Contents

Contents

Acknowledgments

This book was born from *Love*. From my mother's warm embrace, the glow of her smile, her scholarly mind, and her deep laughing journeys with life. From the steady loving kindness of my brother whose wise strength and healing light transformed valleys into spaces of hope. From the breath of my father's ancestral presence, guiding with smiles, showering peace, pride, and protection.

To my mother, the Rev. Naomi O. Harris you have in so many ways breathed life back into my soul. Thank you. In search of your gardens I found my own. Your daughter loves you. To my brother, John Jay A. Harris Jr., thank you for being a deep thinker, a builder of community and an artist of head and heart. You paved a way for my spirit to take flight. Thank you. I believe in you and I love you. I am grateful for you, John A. Harris Sr. for the flow of wisdom that continues to meet me along the river of life. Daddy, I see you. To Sonia Denise, Keith, Alisha, Nathan and Desmond Dozier for being a home for my heart, and to the Harris, Wells, Jones, and Perry families, thank you for pouring your love, laughter, and prayer into this journey.

Friendship like water has nurtured this book from the beginning and lifted me through the process of writing. I accept this as grace in my life and for each gift I am grateful. To my dear friends and sisters, Kate Ott, Jennifer Harvey, Rebecca Todd Peters, Layli Phillips, Davina Lopez, Antoinette Kemp, Regina Dotson, Grace White, and especially, to Cheryl Walker who taught me how to be in the present moment. To the extraordinary mentors who assisted me during the initial phase of this project, Emilie M. Townes, Peter J. Paris, Anthony B. Pinn, Gary Dorrien and Larry Rasmussen. I am especially grateful to Dr. Townes for her consistent support, to Dr. Paris for reading several drafts of this manuscript and to Dr. Larry and Nyla Rasmussen for serving as midwives as I wrote, and wrote, and wrote! There are also those who taught me how to find my voice! For this I wish to thank James H. Cone, Renita J. Weems, James A. and Betty Forbes, John Richard Bryant, Anthony B. Pinn, the late Rev. Jesse Langston Boyd Jr., Rosemarie Harding, Rachel Harding, Vincent Harding, Sheila Davney, Josef Sorett, and the entire Nzinga and Ndugu Family. Compassionate justice found its way into my life through friends whom I wish to thank for supporting me in the life of the mind. These include, Carolyn Medine, Charles Hallisey, Jack Hill, Marcia Y. Riggs, Sharon Watson Fluker, Evelyn Parker, Tonya Burton, William Paul Young, Kaudie McLean, Lori Hartmann, Helen Hunt, Kanyere Eaton, Cecila Boone, Emmanuel Lartey, Joretta Marshall, and Joy Allen.

I could not have completed this work without the support of the faculty and staff of the Religion Department at Texas Christian University. A research leave granted by the Provost, Dr. Newell Donovan, Dean, Andrew Schoolmaster and Chair of the Religion Department, C. David Grant provided me with the opportunity to complete this book. I would also like to thank the faculty of Iliff School of Theology for opening their research doors and hearts to me, and to The Ford Foundation and Womanist Scholars Program under the direction of Dr. Jacquelyn Grant at the Interdominational Theological Center in Atlanta that provided a rich and nurturing environment for me as I was conducting research on this and another writing project. The Wabash Center for Learning and Teaching in Religion and Theology, The Sister Fund, and The Fund for Theological Education have been instrumental partners in my writing journey. I am proud that this work is a part of the powerful Black Religion/Womanist Thought/ Social Justice series at Palgrave Macmillan and am grateful for the vision of series editors Linda Thomas and Dwight Hopkins. Thank you. The gift of a solid and care-filled editor has been a true blessing. Thank you to editor Burke Gerstenschlager for your attention to detail both on and off the page.

To Alice Walker, your life work and words embody the spirit of peace. Thank you for reading this manuscript, for your treasured insights and wisdom. Our connection teaches me so much and I am glad you are pleased with this book. May you continually be touched in heart and mind to be beautiful, inspiring love as the basis for wholeness and community and may we all cherish the Earth divine. To the Spirit—Thank you for giving me voice, courage, and life anew—I love you.

In Peace and Thanksgiving,
MELANIE L. HARRIS

Series Editors' Preface

Melanie L. Harris has written a void-filling book that no one else thought to write. Such an innovative scholarly move indicates both her intellectual creativity and her penetrating insight. What she has skillfully crafted is a text so practically and logically needed. Her claim is convincingly sound. Womanist thought, argues Harris, draws on Alice Walker's phrase "womanist." Until now, womanist theology and ethics have been forged into an American and global discipline by relying on Walker's four-part womanist definition through Walker's fictional prose and poetry. Now Harris (and here is her conceptual breakthrough) pushes us to notice the treasure trove of Walker's nonfictional texts. And then, Harris concludes in a way that is profound by virtue of the fact that others have not thought of it, that is to pose this question: What are the ethical insights of Walker's nonfiction writings and how can these insights be used as sources for a constructive womanist ethics? From the emergence of womanist theology and ethics in the early 1980s until today, no one has really surfaced this query. The gift of Harris is that she asks and answers it.

Unfolding her answer, Harris guides us meticulously through the false oppositional positioning of womanist thought verses black feminist thought. There are shades of differences between these disciplines. However, Harris states compellingly, there exists no sharp dichotomy between the two. In a sense, they both go back to Walker's original definition of "womanist," coined in her 1983 book, *In Search of Our Mothers' Gardens: Womanist Prose*. In fact, the first generation of womanist theologians and ethicists (such as Jacquelyn Grant, Delores Williams, and Katie Cannon—all hailing from Union Theological Seminary in New York City) interchanged theoretical and ethical notions from both womanism and black feminism. Even today, scholars, pastors, and laywomen of both representations draw on intersectional analyses among race, gender, class, sexuality, and (to a degree) ecological justice.

Harris also presents a thorough examination of two womanist foci—deconstruction (i.e., confident encountering and undaunted unveiling of negative practices against black women's lives) and construction (i.e., a multilayered and subtle building of positive human community). And then, scanning the life and thought of Alice Walker, Harris conceptualizes six values and six virtues from the nonfiction texts of Alice Walker's corpus. Harris concludes this book with her own constructive, womanist virtue ethics.

Gifts of Virtue, Alice Walker, and Womanist Ethics is the first book to look at the ethical dimensions of Walker's own nonfiction voice. Womanist thinkers from all walks of life (from ethics to political science and beyond) give praise to Walker as the originator of the theoretical framework for naming womanist creativities. However, womanists have lacked sustained interest in and serious engagement with Walker's nonfictional work that reveals her ethical positions. *Gifts of Virtue, Alice Walker, and Womanist Ethics* deepens the journey into this major aspect of Alice Walker's writings. On that account, among others, this work fits well into the Black Religion/ Womanist Thought/Social Justice Series.

The series publishes both authored and edited manuscripts that have depth, breadth, and theoretical edge and addresses both academic and nonspecialist audiences. It produces works engaging any dimension of black religion or womanist thought as they pertain to social justice. Womanist thought is a new approach in the study of African American women's perspectives. The series includes a variety of African American religious expressions, that is, traditions such as Protestant and Catholic Christianity, Islam, Judaism, Humanism, African Diasporic practices, religion and gender, religion and black gays/lesbians, ecological justice issues, African American religiosity and its relation to African religions, Taoism, Buddhism, Confucionism, new black religious movements (e.g., Daddy Grace, Father Divine or the Nation of Islam), or religious dimensions in African American "secular" experiences (e.g., the spiritual aspects of aesthetic efforts like the Harlem Renaissance and literary giants like James Baldwin, the religious fervor of the Black Consciousness movement, or the religion of compassion in the black women's club movement).

DWIGHT N. HOPKINS, University of Chicago Divinity School
LINDA E. THOMAS, Lutheran School of Theology at Chicago

Introduction

Many said it would not be here. Still. Regardless. And after almost thirty years, womanist theology survives and thrives through the pens, teaching, writing, art, and activism of several waves of womanist religious thought. Birthed out of the minds and critical thinking of such scholars as Katie G. Cannon, Delores S. Williams, Jacquelyn Grant, and Renita J. Weems,[1] womanist theology began with the act of these women boldly naming themselves "womanists," appropriating a term coined by literary writer Alice Walker. Calling sexism a necessary category of contemplation for black Christian traditional churches and demanding black feminist race-class-gender analysis be used in black theological methodology, these women shaped womanist theology and ethics to center the voices and experiences of women of African descent as primary sources for theological reflection.

Womanist theology and ethics made its initial break into academic discourse in 1985 with the publication of an article by Katie G. Cannon entitled "The Emergence of Black Feminist Consciousness," wherein she described how black women scholars in the fields of theology, ethics, biblical studies, and the history and sociology of religion had begun problematizing and critiquing the ways racist, sexist, and classist ideologies were sewn into dominant Christian, feminist, and black liberation theological perspectives.[2] While womanist scholars found some of the theological categories and constructs within dominant Christian perspectives familiar, they argued that in general, black women's perspectives were being left out of various religious discourses and conversations. This posed a problem because in their estimation, black women's experiences of and resistance to racism, classism, and sexism not only influenced their own theological perspectives but also largely informed them. Jacquelyn Grant would explain this point saying, "Black women must do theology out of their tri-dimensional experience of racism/sexism/classism. To ignore any aspect of this experience is to deny the holistic and integrated reality of Black womanhood."[3] The theological lens through which black women examined traditional Christian categories led them to interpret the meaning and significance of certain categories, such as surrogacy and sacrifice, differently and to place less emphasis on some constructs and more on others.[4]

Black women scholars' critique of feminist theological perspectives was complex. They found white feminist methods helpful in uncovering ways in which dominant theological ideas perpetuated gender oppression and agreed with the gender analysis embodied in most feminist perspectives. However, they insisted that feminist theological critique did not go far enough. It fell short in that it did not include racial analysis; thus allowing white feminism to fight against gender oppression while maintaining a heavy layer of racial oppression used against black women and other women of color. On the other hand, racial analysis did play a central role in black male theological perspectives; however, the latter lacked attention to gender analysis.[5] Some black theologies were laden with sexist ideology, and black women scholars found that this fact left black theology open to critiques of sexism. They questioned whether black theology's goal of empowerment for black people included the empowerment of black women. They found it necessary to push black male theologians to incorporate the voices, experiences, and theological perspectives of black women in their ideas of black liberation theology. At the same time, many black women scholars involved in black churches found it imperative to critically assess the role male-dominated theological ideas had in the practice of sexism within black church communities. Many male black church leaders claimed that there were theological and biblical grounds on which to restrict the roles of women in church and limit their opportunities to hold ecclesiastical leadership positions. Calling sexism a necessary category of contemplation for black church leaders and urging that interrelated black feminist race-class-gender analysis be used in the methods, practice, and pedagogy of black liberation thought, this confessional wave of black women scholars moved to establish a new theological perspective, *womanism*, that would center the theological voices and theo-ethical reflections of black women.

Naming themselves "womanists" aligned the project of womanist theology and ethics with the lineage of black women's literature and more specifically with the black woman writer Alice Walker.[6] This alignment would later be identified by Cannon as an interdisciplinary method in womanist ethics and argued as a way of reclaiming the stories of women of African descent as resources for theo-ethical inquiry.

Though the link to the black women's literary tradition was made clear, and the appropriation of Walker's definition of womanist became a basic presupposition for this first wave of womanist scholars, the connection to Alice Walker herself, as an activist and writer, and to the virtues and values that emerged out of her own womanist story was left out.

Alice Walker, a literary scholar and activist who helped to establish and build the study of black women's literary tradition in the 1970s and early 1980s, coined the term "womanist" in order to express the need for black women to name themselves, a part from white women's feminist ideals for them. She also envisioned the term to reconnect black women to black community and to include black men as well, contrary to the separatist attitude held by many white feminists who argued that men could not be involved with a feminist vision.[7] Having been influenced by first-wave feminist ideology but aware of its limited capacity to recognize race, class, and gender as interconnected categories for analysis, Walker defined "womanist" to share some of the same connotations as feminism but to reach beyond its gender-specific lens. Noting the difference between the two schools of thought, Walker wrote, "Womanist is to feminist as purple to lavender," in the fourth part of the definition. According to her, black feminist-oriented women needed to celebrate the moment in time and seize the opportunity to self-name. She envisioned the term "womanist" to reflect community, wholeness, and a radical inclusivity that was ultimately empowering to black women. After initially introducing the term in a 1979 short story entitled "Coming Apart" published in *Take Back the Night*; Walker published the full definition of womanist in her first collection of nonfiction essays, *In Search of Our Mothers' Gardens: Womanist Prose*, in 1983.[8] In its entirety, it reads as follows:

> **Womanist 1.** From *womanish*. (Opp. of "girlish," i.e., frivolous, irresponsible, not serious.) A black feminist or feminist of color. From the black folk expression of mothers to female children, "You acting womanish," i.e., like a woman. Usually referring to outrageous, audacious, courageous or *willful* behavior. Wanting to know more and in greater depth than is considered "good" for one. Interested in grown-up doings. Acting grown up. Being grown up. Interchangeable with another black folk

expression: "You trying to be grown." Responsible. In charge. *Serious.* 2. Also: A woman who loves other women, sexually and/or nonsexually. Appreciates and prefers women's culture, women's emotional flexibility (values tears as natural counterbalance of laughter), and women's strength. Sometimes loves individual men, sexually, and/or nonsexually. Committed to survival and wholeness of entire people, male *and* female. Not a separatist, except periodically, for health. Traditionally universalist, as in: "Mama, why are we brown, pink and yellow and our cousins are white, beige, and black?" Ans: "Well, you know the colored race is just like a flower garden, with every color flower represented." Traditionally capable, as in: "Mama, I'm walking to Canada and I'm taking you and a bunch of other slaves with me." Reply: "It wouldn't be the first time." 3. Loves music. Loves dance. Loves the moon. *Loves* the Spirit. Loves love and food and roundness. Loves struggle. *Loves* the Folk. Loves herself. *Regardless.* 4. Womanist is to feminist as purple to lavender.[9]

Seizing upon Walker's four-part definition of "womanist," black women religious scholars found a word and perspective they could relate to. They found a theoretical framework from which they could develop race-class-gender analysis and shape it into a primary method for religious thought. The work of such black feminists as Barbara Smith, Angela Davis, Paula Giddings, Gloria Wade-Gayles, and bell hooks provided the black feminist theoretical origins,[10] and Cannon, Williams, Grant, Weems, and others adopted their race-class-gender analysis as womanist intersectional analysis to highlight the complex subjectivity of black women and celebrate their religious, theological, and ethical perspectives.

Though there was cause for celebration among the new womanist camp for having found a name that fit, not every black woman religious scholar was receptive or willing to accept the term "womanist." The appropriation of the term "womanist" by womanist Christian theologians and ethicists first became suspect when social ethicist Cheryl J. Sanders critiqued the adoption of a secular term for Christian theological reflection. In her 1989 essay "Roundtable Discussion: Christian Ethics and Theology in Womanist Perspective," Sanders suggests that the lack of "God-language" in the definition was problematic.[11] Sanders's second critique hit the heart of homosexuality debates taking place in black churches and black culture. She claimed that the reference to lesbianism in Walker's definition barred womanist Christian theologians and ethicists from using the term for any sort of valid biblical and moral Christian analysis.

"Sanders' article moved many womanists and feminists scholars to react. The responses included "waves of anger" from Cannon as

she tried to engage the bases of Sanders' argument as a fellow ethicist; a critique that Sanders had misread Walker's treatment of lesbianism launched by Emilie M. Townes; and a reminder from M.
Shawn Copeland for Sanders and others to use careful citations in
their writing to push womanism into formal academic discourse.
These were the first three responses to Sanders.[12] They were followed
by responses from bell hooks concerning the "Christian" separation
between black feminism and womanism and the acknowledgment
by Cheryl Townsend Gilkes that although Walker did not identify as
Christian, Gilkes believed the term to still be powerful and useful to
create space for black women in the academy." These echoes and their
continued effect on the shaping and making of womanist thought
make further consideration of Sanders's critiques worthwhile.

Although most womanist theologians and ethicists at the time wrote
from a Christian perspective, many refused to acknowledge that the
word "womanist" is hardly Christian-based. The term is not inherently
theistic, nor Christian, but rather emphasizes a secular philosophical
stance for black women's self-assertion and self-definition. In her essay,
Sanders questions the appropriateness of the term "womanist" not only
because the term is secular (and, therefore, for her, not a legitimate
foundation on which to base black women's theological and ethical
thought) but also because Walker herself may not have intended for the
term to be used for solely Christian dialogue; rather, for here Walker
would have likely meant to uplift the spiritualities and religious sensibilities of women of African descent everywhere. Sanders suggests that
as a literary writer, Walker herself did not intend for "womanist" to
be developed into a theoretical tool or labeled a Christian theological
perspective describing black women's belief systems. Although Walker
probably did not preclude womanist theologians or theological ethicists from using the term (if it proved helpful toward unleashing black
women's voices), Sanders suggests, she did not intend for the term to
become an avenue for Christian theological and ethical work.

In the "Roundtable Discussion," Sanders reasons that the lack of
"God-language" in the definition is additional proof that the term is
secular and warns that those using the term for Christian theological
reflection should be hesitant to do so.

> The fact is that womanist is essentially a secular cultural category whose
> theological and ecclesial significations are rather tenuous.... Walker's
> definition comprises an implicit ethics of moral autonomy, libera-
> tion, sexuality and love that is not contingent upon the idea of God or
> revelation.[13]

Even the phrase "loves the spirit" in the definition, Sanders says, is not enough to illustrate the presence of the "sacred" in the expression "womanist." Rather, Sanders uses the imagery of "the mule" represented in Zora Neale Hurston's work as a metaphor to describe the offspring of womanists' heaving efforts to produce Christian theological scholarship out of the seed of a secular term.

Sanders's second concern with womanist theologians and ethicists appropriating Walker's womanist definition surrounds Walker's embrace of women's sexuality and the inclusion of lesbianism. For Sanders, it is problematic for black Christian women feminist theologians and ethicists to accept Walker's description of the term because the reference to sexual orientation outside of heterosexual existence is immoral, unbiblical, and, therefore, un-Christian. Following the responses given by several noted womanist theologians and ethicists and black feminists in the "Roundtable Discussion,"[14] Sanders writes some final remarks about her specific denominational location and point of view on lesbianism. She admits her beliefs and church doctrine as a member, teacher, and minister in the Church of God heavily influence her opinion about embracing homosexuality and, therefore, fuel her argument against using the term "womanist."

> After giving careful consideration to their concerns and objectifications...I became aware of an important factor that I did not explicitly raise in my statement but that does influence my thought and convictions on these issues. As a member of the Church of God...I identify very closely with the holiness tradition....I suspect that my identification with the holiness tradition, perhaps more than any other factor, accounts for my position on these two issues, i.e., my insistence upon making hard and fast distinctions between the sacred and the secular in theory, and my deep concern for the moral significance of sexual norms in praxis.[15]

Sanders's critique of womanist theologians and ethicists for using the term "womanist" is based on the Christian-centered and church-based analysis she indicates is crucial to recovering black women's experiences of religion. She argues that the term's secular orientation and reference to lesbianism make it problematic for black women Christian scholars to embody the fullness of Walker's definition. Sanders also suggests that methodologies used in the discourse are too closely connected to a Christian, conservative perspective (especially on the issue of homosexuality) to conduct adequate analysis using all four areas (race, gender, class, and sexual orientation) represented in Walker's definition. Sanders's thoughts about the appropriation of "womanist" can be summed up in her question to womanists: "Are we committing a gross conceptual error when we use Walker's descriptive cultural nomenclature as a foundation for the normative discourse of theology and ethics?"[16]

Walker's Womanism

After almost thirty years in the academy, womanist theological and ethical scholarship has now reached a level of academic maturity whereby Sanders's critiques and others sparked by third-wave womanist, feminist, and black theology are now being fully examined and embraced. Questions concerning the absence of citations from Walker's nonfiction in womanist theological scholarship, the avoidance of dialogue about Walker's own spiritual path, and the evasion of Walker's nonfiction ethical voice are some of the issues raised in the new debate about the nature of womanist methodology and theological inquiry.

No Alice

Excluding the voice of Alice Walker in womanist religious discourse appears to be a peculiar mark of womanist methodology. Contrary to Sanders's approach in the "Roundtable Discussion" to go straight to the source of Walker's work, most present-day womanist theological writers vacillate between whether to incorporate Walker's work and perspective on spiritual or theological issues. One reason for this may be Walker's fluid spirituality. Describing this to interviewer Scott Winn, Walker explains, "I'm probably tri-spiritual. I was raised as a Christian. Now I love Buddhism and I love earth religion."[17] Walker expands upon her connection to Earth-spiritualities in the preface of the tenth-anniversary edition of *The Color Purple*.[18] Reflecting back, she says,

> Whatever else *The Color Purple* has been...it remains for me the theological work examining the journey from the religious back to the spiritual....Having recognized myself as a worshiper of Nature by the age of eleven, because my spirit resolutely wandered out the window to find trees and wind during Sunday sermons, I saw no reason why, once free, I should bother with religious matters at all.[19]

In this quote, Walker defines herself as a worshiper of nature and in her later essays, describes a worshipper of nature to be pagan. However, traditional Christian definitions associate demonarchy with paganism. If womanist theological methodologies have been influenced by these traditional Christian assumptions, then one reason Walker's pagan and nonfiction ethical voice may be neglected in womanist thought is the belief that paganism as devoted to the earth, is some how anti-Christian. Although Walker holds a place for the figure of Jesus in her theology,[20] Christian womanist methodologies may inherently limit conversation with Walker's voice (or any other theological dialogue partner who does not share the same theological understanding and common beliefs) because of the perceived threat that paganism poses to established Christian theology.[21] That is to say, methodologies used in womanist religious thought, because of their connection with Christianity and the institutional black church, may be shaped to exclude the voice of Walker because she represents a non-Christian perspective.

When asked at a womanist conference if Walker's paganism banned womanist Christian theologians and ethicists from using Walker's own work and religious stance, acclaimed womanist M. Shawn Copeland argued that Walker's personal beliefs were of no consequence to the appropriation of "womanist." "It never bothers me. The point is does she say something that rings true? And does that make a contribution to furthering the truth that we see? And if that happens, I'm not that very much interested in the role of her [Walker's] religion...on a personal level."[22] Proof that variations of this opinion are shared among other Christian womanist ethicists and theologians can be found in the limited reference to Walker's nonfiction work in womanists' theological texts.[23]

The fact the Walker's personal non-Christian and pagan stance is irrelevant to womanist Christian theologians and ethicists appropriating the term in 2004 reinvokes Sanders's 1989 critique about womanist authority. "On what grounds, if any, can womanist authority and authenticity be established in our work?"[24] The act of appropriating the term with little regard for Walker's own spiritual stance or nonfiction work suggests that even as the mother of the term, Walker holds no authority to help determine the nature of womanist thought. Nor does she have any say in how womanist Christian theologians and ethicists use the word "womanist." Beyond her contribution of the definition, Walker's voice doesn't seem to be important to the development of womanist theological debate. The question of authority in womanist theological thought is worth exploration; however, that subject falls outside of the scope of this book. That Walker's nonfiction ethical voice is not referenced in womanist Christian theological and ethical work is the background against which this book undertakes to recover the resource of Walker's nonfiction work as evidence of her ethical system; one worthy of womanist ethical study.

If, indeed, Walker is too pagan or too spiritually fluid to be a womanist, then the methodologies and Christian theological presuppositions that make up womanist theological thought must be examined. Alice Walker is a black woman. And womanist religious thought at its core is dedicated to expressing the ethical visions and voices of black women. Walker, then, should be neither cut out of her own definition nor banished from womanist religious thought. Rather, her identity as a black woman, a writer, and a practitioner of fluid spirituality should make a path for her to plant flowers in her own garden.

Conflicts in Method

The act of silencing Walker's nonfiction ethical voice in womanist theological work may be the result of methodologies used in womanist theological scholarship. For further discussion, it is helpful to return to Sanders's "Roundtable Discussion" critique. One of the significant contributions of the "Roundtable Discussion" held by Sanders, other womanist theologians and ethicists, and black feminists is the model it provides for careful analysis of Walker's actual words and work. This careful analysis can be seen as a methodological step Sanders takes of "going to the source."

Sanders's inclusion of Walker's nonfiction voice by pointing to Walker's essay "Gifts of Power" while discussing lesbianism is a significant move for womanist scholarship.[25] The methodological step of going to the source—Alice Walker's work—seems to be Sanders's approach to developing an argument against using "womanist" for Christian theological reflection. At the same time, however, I contend that Sanders's approach of going directly to the source is an attempt, perhaps without prior knowledge, to uncover the rich, raw resources of black women's writings and stories for womanist theological and theo-ethical reflection. Due to Sanders's inclusion of Walker's work in the roundtable discussion, other womanists and black feminists responding in the article also incorporate Walker's work. This move to incorporate Walker's own nonfiction voice seldom occurs in womanist theological scholarship. Reference to Walker's fiction work is more common. *The Color Purple*, characters in *The Third Life of Grange Copeland*, and other fiction works are clearly cited by womanist theologians and ethicists writing from a Christian theological perspective.[26] The exception to this rule is Katie Cannon, who has used Walker's nonfiction work extensively in her research on the historical figure of Zora Neale Hurston.[27] Still, in light of the fact that Walker coined the term "womanist," the move to overlook Walker's own nonfiction work is problematic. Negating the importance of Walker's nonfiction work exposes a significant gap in the discipline of womanist ethics, whose important and fundamental task is uncovering the voices of women of African descent. This is also the key task of womanist religious thought. According to womanist ethicist Marcia Y. Riggs, the primary goal of womanist ethics is to "uncover" black women's experiences, lives, and stories as key resources for theological and religious reflection. Riggs articulates this and other goals in her book *Awake, Arise & Act: A Womanist Call to Black Liberation.*[28] She writes,

> Womanists engage in at least four tasks: a) uncovering the roots of a womanist tradition through examination and reintegration of black women's experience into black history in particular and American history in general; b) debunking social myths so as to undermine the black woman's acceptance of sexist oppression, the black man's acceptance of patriarchal privilege and the white woman's acceptance of white racist privilege; c) constructing black womanist theology and religious ethics in light of the first two tasks and to broaden these disciplines to include nontraditional bases and sources for theological and ethical reflection; d) envisioning human liberation (not solely racial/ethnic-group or gender-group liberation) under God; that is, black womanists are proposing a decidedly inclusive perspective that is acutely aware of the need for the simultaneous liberation from all oppression.[29]

Riggs's task of "uncovering the roots of a womanist tradition" suggests that studying the lives and ethical thought of historical and present-day black women is crucial for womanist scholarship. This being the case, Sanders's methodological move to go to the source of Walker's ethical voice embedded in her nonfiction work is helpful.

Going to the Source

Sanders is not the only scholar who would have suggested or been privy to the methodological move to go to the source of experiences, stories, and lives of women of African descent. In fact, this move is characteristic of a number of liberation theologies, including feminist theology and black liberation theology. Beginning with experience and narrative—validating these as important sources for theological inquiry and mining them for religious categories—is a classical methodological strategy to uncover previously silenced or marginalized voices. In the task of uncovering Walker's voice for the creation and practice of womanist religious thought, there is a womanist ethical method previously established and familiar to womanist approaches that helps set the stage to go directly to the source of Walker's nonfiction work to uncover virtues and values helpful in constructing a womanist virtue ethic. Katie Cannon's ethical method, as she describes it in her groundbreaking work *Black Womanist Ethics*, establishes the first frames for womanist virtue and helps chart a pathway back into womanist gardens in order to hear the ethical nonfiction voice of Walker, thereby uncovering her valuable contributions to womanist ethics. In addition to providing a list of rich virtues and values that can serve as guiding principles in life, examination of Walker's work suggests a method that highlights the perspectives and voices of many women of African descent, thus prompting Christian womanist ethicists to open their eyes and expand the boundaries of their thought to incorporate interreligious and interdisciplinary dialogue, as well as focus on the global links and common worldviews shared among women of African descent and their communities.

In this book, I construct a womanist virtue ethic consisting of values derived from Walker's own ethic and virtues gleaned from her nonfiction essays. To do this, I adopt Cannon's womanist ethical method and highlight experiential themes in selected essays by Walker. Next, I glean ethical implications and sift values from these themes. In some cases, Walker herself clearly names values that guide her own ethic and illustrates for the reader how her analysis of her mother's story and other women's stories signals particular values helpful for establishing a healthy mode of being and ethical way of living in the world. In other essays, the ethical implications signaled in Walker's writing are offered as a resource from which virtues for the construction of a womanist virtue ethic can be gleaned. This introductory chapter argues for the importance of including Walker's ethical voice in the discourse of womanist religious thought. Chapter 1 offers a biographical study of Walker's life. The inclusion of this moral biography is in keeping with the womanist ethical task of uncovering black women's stories and highlighting their experience as an important source for their moral framework. The chapter focuses on three phases of Walker's life: her birth and childhood, her early activist and college years, and her mothering and professional writing years. This extensive chapter describes the people, important events, and social movements and communities that contributed to the shaping of Walker's virtues and values and thus informed her ethic.

Concentrating on the analysis of Walker's writings, chapter 2 explicates the use and adaptation of Cannon's method as a way of engaging selected nonfiction essays by Walker in order to glean virtues and values from her work. Chapter 3 begins the work of the first step of the method, identifying experiential themes from which ethical implications can be gleaned and values in Walker's ethic determined. Examination of Walker's own approach of gleaning values from the stories of women of African descent as well as her own mother's story is the focus of chapter 4. Here, I also discuss the values that Walker adopts as important resources for ethical living. The values include mutuality in relationship, communal interdependence, self-reliance, and letting go for the sake of survival. With these values uncovered, chapter 5 summarizes a list of core virtues that serve to construct a womanist virtue ethic. These virtues—generosity, graciousness, compassion, spiritual wisdom, audacious courage, justice, and good community—are each explicated in this chapter that concludes with the summary of a womanist virtue ethic.

Chapter 6 introduces third-wave womanism as a distinct wave that expands womanist religious thought and methodologies to further embody a threefold objective that stretches the discipline beyond the traditional boundaries of womanism. The first objective is to argue for womanist study that celebrates a variety of religious traditions that are life affirming and life giving to women of African descent and their communities. A second task for third-wave womanism is to build up and give attention to the global links within the body of womanism. This includes highlighting the significance of African women's theologies for womanist scholarship and uncovering methodological connections between African womanist literary theory and interdisciplinary methods used by African American womanist scholars. A third task is to face critiques launched by other discourses as a way of expanding womanist discourse and critically engaging womanist ideas in conversation with other points of view, that is, to encourage interdisciplinary study in religion, ethics, and theology.

The Epilogue summarizes the major contributions of Walker's work for womanist ethics. In addition to being a model of social activism, Walker's novels, nonfiction, and poetry continue to be a source of inspiration to people throughout the globe who are searching for a better way of life and the morals and values that accompany it. This lens into Walker's moral life is one way to identify religious and social values that will facilitate peace and social justice by the shaping and habitual practice of life-affirming values. .

As womanist religious thought celebrates almost thirty years in the academy, new approaches are being shaped and developed to expand the reach of womanist religious thought and to widen womanist perspectives across disciplines, across religions, and across the globe. This work builds upon the premise of womanism that believes black women's voices, lives, and experiences are valid sources for theological and ethical inquiry. It also reminds womanist artists, activists, writers, and academicians of the various gifts, survival strategies, modes of wholeness, and values that contribute to thriving in life, that come from sharing stories that liberate and produce transformative and ethical guides for living.

"A Womanist Story": Alice Walker's Moral Biography

The life of Alice Walker is more than a collection of historical events and memories. It is, rather, a rich orchestra of people, movements, morals, values, personal achievements, and societal transformations that have shaped the personhood and life orientation of this well-known author. This chapter takes a biographical look at three phases of Walker's life in a way that highlights the development of her values and directs our focus on some of the life experiences that shaped her morals and ethical sensibilities as an activist and writer. The three phases discussed here are Walker's birth and childhood, her early activist and college years, and her mothering and professional writing years. A brief survey of the selected nonfiction books that I use as sources from which to glean virtues and values from Walker is also included in this chapter.

Beginnings

Born in 1944 in Eatonton, Georgia, Walker was the eighth child of Millie Lou and Willie Lee Walker. The couple married during the Great Depression and together endured a life of sharecropping while raising their eight children.[1] The Walker family survived through three significant phases of American history: the Great Depression, the Jim Crow era, and the Civil Rights Movement. Survival, it seems, is just one value that the Walkers possessed as a part of their family heritage.

As with many people of African descent living in North America, the Walker family story begins on the continent of Africa, where

African peoples were ripped from their motherland, captured, chained, and forced into slave ships carrying them from the shores of their native home to the "New World" beginning in the 1600s. More than two centuries later, with the laws of slavery still in place, the oldest known relative in the Walker family, Mary Poole, was forced to move from Virginia to Eatonton, Georgia as part of the slave trade. Poole lived during the 1800s as a slave and witnessed the Civil War, Emancipation, and Reconstruction. Poole is remembered by Alice Walker in many of her essays, including one written in tribute to Martin Luther King Jr. entitled "Choice: A Tribute to Martin Luther King, Jr." In this essay, Walker reminds her readers of King's ability to reconnect black people to themselves and to their ancestral land of the South, and she notes the important gift King inspired in her to remember her own roots and heritage. Of Mary Poole she writes, "My great-great-great-grandmother walked as a slave from Virginia to Eatonton, Georgia—which passes for the Walker ancestral home—with two babies on her hips. She lived to be a hundred and twenty-five years old and my own father knew her as a boy."[2] The intergenerational connection between Walker's great-great-great-grandmother and Walker's father in the essay suggests that the value of memory and the ability to recall the names of family ancestors is very important to Walker. Coinciding with her commitment to the values of being a black Southern writer, Walker's writings about Mary Poole and the use of family stories in her work are a way of uncovering the stories and voices of women who have previously been silenced.

Walker's award-winning essay "In Search of Our Mothers' Gardens" is a key instructive example of this point.[3] Here, she not only gives the names of women who have inspired and paved a way for her writing but also alludes to the fact that there are countless women of African descent who have inspired her and others to take up the pen. Walker implies that it behooves any woman of African descent living in the present to honor the women of the past, who may have never been allowed to write because they were sharecroppers or slaves but who had every bit of intelligence and creativity to do so. Acknowledging the value of ancestors and honoring the memory of those who could not write by recording their stories are elements of Walker's writing style and a form of practice that shows up in her method of uncovering the voices and experiences of black women's lives and beliefs. Walker's act of recalling the name of Mary

Poole is one way of honoring her own ancestors and carrying on their hope in her memory.

Home

For more than one hundred years, the Walker family has called Eatonton home.[4] Claiming this title on the basis of her ancestors' spiritual and physical connection to the land as sharecroppers and former slaves, Walker explains that while the racist laws of the segregated South prohibited her family from owning the land they faithfully worked and tilled it for generations. The grave markers that serve as a final resting place for her loved ones are proof that "the land of my birthplace belongs to me, dozens of times over."[5] This move to reclaim birthplace and reestablish home illustrates major themes in Walker's writings that surface as significant values expressed throughout her nonfiction work. She writes extensively about the values of belonging, having a place to call one's own, and home in relation to black peoples' agony of having been ripped from their ancestral land of Africa, and the sheer strength and courage it took to rebuild a place for themselves in the United States. Making slave quarters, squat houses, and huts home required great emotional, psychological, and spiritual strength from black and African slaves. It was the tremendous respect that they had for the Earth and nature that enabled them to pour their physical labor into the soil to harvest crops. Even as they knew that the best of what was produced from the Earth would not be made available to the slaves themselves, but rather given to the slave owners' family. Being forced to work the land holding deep respect for it and its rich resources for health and well-being presented a tension within the story of African people's relationship with land. Walker discusses some of this tension in her essay "The Only Reason You Want to Go to Heaven" and elaborates on the importance of the sacred relationship that black people have with land.[6] She also notes, in her tribute to King, how significant land is to their sense of home.[7] Perhaps most important to her biography is the significance of her ancestors' story with land, uncovered in interviews between Walker and Evelyn C. White.

The history of owning and having that land taken away from the Walker family because of their race is important to uncovering Walker's spiritual value of the Earth. It also serves as a opening through which to explore Walker's sense of environmental justice or ecowomanist perspective that places emphasis on the sense of belonging and home. According to family history, Alice Walker's sense of connection to the land begins with the story of Albert Walker, her paternal great-grandfather, who inherited land from his Scottish slaveholding father and became a successful cotton farmer.[8] When a series of boll weevil plagues destroyed crops of Albert Walker, who had years of success in growing and harvesting, he and his family were left with nothing. The impact of land theft and other forms of systematic disenfranchisement such as violent lynchings were all attempts to destroy the very spirit of the Walker family. The loss was very hard. Having arisen out of the depths of facing violence everyday, to being considered an affluent black family, Albert Walker was now forced to live without the economic security he once had and was forced to endure ridicule and humiliation from white landowners who had been jealous of his success.

Readjusting to a life without privilege proved especially painful for Albert Walker's son, Henry Clay Walker, who was raised to expect a wealthy lifestyle. White's biography captures a glimpse of how the dispossession of land affected Henry Clay Walker and impacted later generations. Bill Walker (Alice Walker's brother) recalls how his grandfather struggled to get over the heartbreak of losing the socio-economic status he was born into. " 'Pa-Pa' was spoiled because he had grown up like a rich kid, riding around on horses and wearing fancy clothes...so when my great-grandfather Albert lost his land, Pa-Pa couldn't deal with them having to scuffle and scrape like regular people. He started drinking, gambling and hanging out in jook joints. He got a real bad reputation."[9]

Regardless of his loss of wealth, "bad reputation," and the rumors about him that circulated among black and white society crowds, Estella "Shug" Perry, a woman of questionable reputation among the society crowds, fell in love with Henry. They began a love affair that would later be lived out in Alice Walker's fictional account of the relationship between Mister (Albert) and Shug Avery in *The Color Purple*. In real life, the love affair was short lived. Henry's mere attraction to Shug Perry angered his father, Albert Walker, who was at the time doing all he could to rebuild his family's wealth and maintain what little they had left. Albert forbade Henry from seeing Shug because of her reputation. "The Walker family despised Shug Perry because she was considered a loose woman...my great-grandfather Albert was determined to get Henry out of her clutches,"[10] Bill Walker later revealed in an interview. So, having convinced his son that Shug Perry was not the kind of woman Henry would be allowed to marry, Albert persuaded him to marry Kate Nelson. Kate

Nelson was born to a "respectable" family but would never be the woman Henry truly loved; and in time, he beat her senselessly, taking out his shame and anger on her body, a living target of Henry's abuse.

Readers familiar with Walker's novel *The Color Purple* will note the similarities between Henry Clay Walker, Shug Perry, and Kate Nelson and the fictional characters Mr.___ , Shug Avery, and Celie. The book is actually premised on the family story between Henry Clay Walker, Shug Perry, and Rachel Walker, the young wife Henry married after Kate was murdered. Alice Walker secured the plot of *The Color Purple* based on an event Annie Ruth. Walker's witnessed when observing Rachel admire a pair of pink panties that Shug Perry had on. When Rachel asked if she could have them (because she had nothing that nice), Shug simply gave them to her in an act of kindness.[11]

It was the son of Henry and Kate, Willie Lee Walker, Alice Walker's father, born on September 9, 1909, who would grow up shielding his mother and his other siblings from his father's abuse. Seeing no need to be faithful to a wife he did not love, Henry pursued other women (including Shug Perry) throughout his marriage to Kate. The extrafamilial liaisons led to heartbreak and a retributive affair between Kate Nelson Walker and a murderously jealous lover. According to family members, the man was so jealous that when Kate tried to cut the affair off, he showed up and pointed a gun at her. White's biography recounts the story best.

> On July 4, 1921, while walking home from an outing with her son Willie Lee, Kate was accosted by her former lover, who reputedly stepped from behind a bush, pistol in hand. When she rebuffed his pleas to "keep company" again, he poked the gun in her chest and it fired. Kate Nelson Walker died the next day, a month shy of her thirtieth birthday.[12]

Having witnessed the murder of his mother at age eleven, Willie Lee would live the rest of his life with the memory of trying to save his mother as she lay dying on the road bleeding to death. Years later, the trauma and reflection of his mother would revisit him in the face of his second youngest daughter, Annie Ruth. In Walker's nonfiction essay entitled "Father," she writes of how her sister Annie Ruth looked like and "had similar expressions" to that of her grandmother Kate. In the essay, Walker explains how the trauma of witnessing his mother's death had a negative contagious impact on Willie Lee's ability to bond with his own children—especially Annie Ruth.

> My father was so confused that when my sister Ruth appeared in the world and physically resembled his mother, and sounded like his mother, and had similar expressions, he rejected her and missed no opportunity that I ever saw to put her down. I, of course, took the side of my sister, forfeiting my chance to be my father's favorite among the...children.[13]

She did not know it at the time she was growing up, but Walker's willful attitude toward her father mirrored the attitude of her mother, Minnie Lou, who directed courageous and independent behavior toward her own father, William A. Grant. According to a family interview, "Minnie Lou...locked horns with her father, never hesitating to confront him whenever he launched into one of his violent rampages....She'd get all up in his face and tell him what a lowdown, rotten, no-count husband and father he was."[14]

Minnie Tallulah (Lou) Grant was born on December 2, 1912. She was the fifth of twelve children in her family and at an early age became an ardent protector of her mother, Nettie Lee, who also suffered from abuse at the hands of her husband. By the time Minnie Lou was seventeen, she decided, against the will of her father, to take the direction of her life into her own hands. She fell in love with Willie Lee Walker and began strategizing on how to get out of her father's house. "She got pregnant. That guaranteed that her father would put her out. Then she could do what she wanted to do."[15] Minnie Lou Grant and Willie Lee Walker were married on June 1, 1930. They began their lives together, leaving behind the homes they grew up in but carrying with them tragic and triumphant memories, stories, and values that would cultivate the Walker family heritage. It was into this heritage that Alice Walker was born.

Birth

By the time Alice Malsenior (named after two aunts)[16] was born in 1944, the Walker family had seven children, the oldest of which was already working independently from the family and living on his own.[17] Willie Lee and Minnie Lou moved their family twice in search of better wages as sharecroppers; yet they lived in poverty. Nevertheless, Walker explains that her family always had provisions—enough to survive—and never allowed their economic status to diminish their own self-worth. "We knew, I suppose, that we were poor but we never considered ourselves to be poor, unless, of course, we were deliberately humiliated. And because we never believed we were poor, and therefore worthless, we could depend on one another without shame."[18]

The reality of the unjust system of sharecropping in the South made believing in one's worth and depending upon each other necessary values. Sharecropping, often described as the second phase of slavery, required black and poor white Southern farmers to lease land from wealthy white landowners and use their own labor and harvest as payment for the use of the land. Unfair rules and excessive charges made the opportunity for sharecroppers to turn a profit off of their work and the goal of feeding their families next to impossible. Practically everything they grew or made a profit from went directly to the landowner.

Walker describes sharecropping as a system "in which a relatively few ruling class white people had the possibility of having as much food, land, space and cheap energy to run their enterprises as they wanted, while most people of color and many poor white people had barely enough of anything to keep themselves alive."[19] The individual, or small family, simply could not survive on its own. Therefore, community established through borrowing, sharing, and exchanging became the key to surviving.

This same value of community became a central theme in Walker's birth story. At the time Alice was born, the Walkers were making only between two and three hundred dollars a year.[20] In the context of the stress of having seven young mouths to feed and raise properly and the pressure of providing an education for each of them, Minnie Lou's eighth pregnancy was a surprise. The Walkers never expected another child and certainly knew they couldn't afford to have one. Walker would later reflect on her birth story, empathizing with the stress her parents must have felt as they prepared to bring an eighth child into the world. "My birth, the eighth child, unplanned, must have elicited more anxiety than joy. It hurts me to think that for both my parents, poor people, my arrival represented many more years of backbreaking and spirit-crushing toil."[21]

Still, there was an element of pride in Walker's coming into the family. Her birth was the first time her parents could afford to pay the midwife cash for her services. Previously, as was the custom among poor Southerners practicing the value of community, the services of the midwife were given in exchange for whatever the family could afford, for example, food from the fields or a farm animal. In a poem entitled "Three Dollars Cash," Walker commemorates her birth as a symbolic moment of success and financial stability for her family.[22] The poem also reemphasizes the value of radical mutuality between community members and the importance of community instilled in Walker from her beginning and practiced throughout her life.[23]

Childhood

> Alice was a very alert baby...we could all tell, by the way her eyes took in everything, that she was going to be special.[24]

This memory of Walker's birth from neighbor and teacher Miss Birda Reynolds is reflective of the way many people in the Wards Chapel community felt about Walker's entry into the world. As the member of a well-loved and admired family, Walker was quite naturally adopted as a "favorite baby" in the community and was expected to exhibit all and more of the intelligence her older siblings had shown in school. Years after Walker stepped foot into her first-grade classroom (a full year ahead of the other children), Miss Reynolds remembered Walker's early learning years, "A lot of children passed my way, but Alice Walker was the smartest one I ever had."[25]

Even from a young age, Walker dreamed of becoming a writer. According to her family members, Walker's desire to write first manifested itself in her passion for reading. Stories told by her older sister, Annie Ruth, reveal that even as a toddler, Walker would "back herself up against a wall and pretend to read the Sears and Roebuck catalogue."[26] By the time she was four, Walker was doing more than pretending. Miss Reynolds recalls that "from day one, she could out spell children twice her age. And if she had to recite a nursery rhyme or a verse of poetry, Alice didn't get nervous. She'd get up, recite perfectly and sit back down. Lord yes, she had the stuff from the beginning."[27]

Knowing her "stuff" as a child and expressing her joyous personality were easy for Walker to do in the classroom. However, receiving a quality education as a black girl, raised in the segregated South, was no small feat. Segregation laws built along the untrue premise of "separate but equal" required black children to be educated in classrooms far less equipped and with far fewer books than designated for white children being educated in the South. In addition, most black children belonging to sharecropping families did not get the opportunity to focus solely on school work. Most rich white landowners saw little sense in blacks receiving education and instead reasoned that they should be working in the fields, "as soon as their tiny fingers could grasp a cotton ball and drop it into a croker sack."[28] Mrs. Minnie Lou Walker saw things altogether differently. White's biography records how hard Mrs. Walker had to fight to make sure all of her children received an education.

> Indeed, she was known throughout Putnam County for her bold reply to a white plantation owner who, asserting that blacks had "no need for education," had once tried to bully her into sending her children to the fields. "You might have some black children somewhere," Mrs. Walker told the man as she stood, steely eyed, on her front porch, "but they don't live in this house. Don't you ever come around here again talking about how my children don't need to learn how to read and write."[29]

Strong willed and determined, Walker's father also felt strongly about making sure his children received a quality education. In her essay entitled "Father," Walker recounts the distant relationship she had with her father while he was living but recalls that one way in which he showed his affection and the one thing she was sure about was that he believed in education for his children.[30] In fact, it was Willie Lee Walker who led a working campaign to build a new school house for black children in the Wards Chapel community. He argued that the old, rundown, segregated school house the school board provided needed to be replaced with a better one, whether they approved of it or not. So, for several months, after a full day's work of backbreaking labor in the fields, women and men in the community would gather to work through the night hauling materials from an old barracks to build the new school house. When the school opened in 1948, Alice Walker was one of the first children to experience a new space for education in the warmth of the community and witness the incredible results of communal work. The new school house was not only a symbol of pride signifying the value of education in the community, but was also a place in which children felt secure from the external forces of poverty and racism. "There was such security in knowing they were building a place for us," Walker later recalled.[31]

Since education was a key priority in the Walkers' community and household, Walker's dreams to become a writer were nurtured. But in the end, it was not only her family's valuing education that served as the impetus for her learning but also an "accident" that led to Walker's entray into the world of words.

"Accident"

> I am eight years old and a tomboy. I have a cowboy hat, cowboy boots, checkered shirt and pants, all red. My playmates are my brothers, two and four years older than I.... On Saturday nights we all go to the picture show....Back home, "on the ranch," we pretend we are Tom Mix, Hopalong Cassidy, Lash LaRue...we chase each other for hours rustling cattle, being outlaws, delivering damsels from distress. Then my parents decide to buy my brothers guns. These are not "real" guns. They shoot "BBs," copper pellets my brothers say will kill birds. Because I am a girl, I do not get a gun. Instantly I am relegated to the position of Indian. Now there appears to be a distance between us. They shoot and shoot at everything with their new guns. I try to keep up with my bow and arrows.
>
> One day while I am standing on top of our makeshift "garage"— pieces of tin nailed across some poles—holding my bow and arrow and looking out towards the fields, I feel an incredible blow in my right eye. I look down in time to see my brother lower his gun.
>
> Both brothers rush to my side. My eye stings, and I cover it with my hand. "If you tell," they say, "we will get a whipping. You don't want that to happen, do you?" I do not. "Here is a piece of wire," says the older brother, picking it up from the roof; "say you stepped on one end of it and the other flew up and hit you." The pain is beginning to start. "Yes," I say. "Yes, I will say that is what happened." If I do not say this is what happened, I know my brothers will find ways to make me wish I had. But now I will say anything that gets me to my mother...
>
> I am in shock...but it is really how I look that bothers me most. Where the BB pellet struck there is a glob of whitish scar tissue, a hideous cataract, on my eye. Now when I stare at people...they stare back. Not at the "cute" little girl, but at her scar. For six years I do not stare at anyone, because I do not raise my head.[32]

The trauma of being shot by her brother and being coerced into lying about it in order to absolve her brothers of any responsibility would have lifelong consequences for Walker. When the truth that Curtis and Bobby were responsible for the shooting became known, it was too late. The damage had already been done to Walker's physical, emotional, and psychological being. At eight years old, Walker was blind in one eye, and the disfiguration of that eye, the result of a "hideous cataract," would greatly impact her self-esteem and profoundly change her self-perception and personality. "I'm ugly. Everybody knows I'm not pretty anymore" was how Walker described herself to a childhood friend, Doris Reid, at the time. Reid, who witnessed the transformation in Walker's personality, recalls, "Before, Alice was inquisitive and extremely outgoing...after the accident, she wanted to be more alone. She tended to be more to herself...spend a lot more time with her books."[33]

As Walker became more withdrawn from her community in Milledgeville where the shooting occurred, her parents attempted to bring her back into her old joyous self, but even their best efforts backfired. In desperation, the Walkers decided to send Alice to her grandparents, Rachel and Henry Walker in Ward's Chapel in hopes that the healing grace shown by community members and teachers would help bring Alice back to life. However, young Walker would interpret the separation from her parents, sisters, and brothers as punishment. Later, as an adult, she would describe that phase of her life as being compounded with a sense of betrayal and abandonment.

> The unhappy truth is that I was left feeling a great deal of pain and loss and forced to think I had somehow brought it on myself. It was very [much] like a rape. It was the first time I abandoned myself, by lying, and is at the root of my fear of abandonment. It is also the root of my need to tell the truth, always, because I experienced, very early, the pain of telling a lie.[34]

Only much later in her life did Walker come to know more of the truth of why her family reacted in that way. Although, it seemed that they had sent her away, a few months after the shooting, Mr. and Mrs. Walker decided to move their entire family from Milledgeville, to Ward's Chapel to follow Alice. It wasn't until Alice was an adult that she was able to process this move as a deep act of love from her family. She writes, "I now understand that my parents moved the entire family back to known territory partly to follow me! I am so sorry I was so late understanding this love."[35]

New Sight

Thirty-one years would pass before Alice Walker ever wrote publicly about her eye injury in 1952. During that time, she became an award-winning writer and poet, a teacher, a civil rights worker, a social activist, a wife, and a mother. It was this latter identity of mother that first allowed Walker to break her silence and write about her eye injury and release full emotional healing back into her life with new insight into her work.

In "Beauty: When the Other Dancer Is the Self," Walker recounts the details of the accident in 1952 by using a flashback literary style, by which the reader is told the story through the narrative of certain moments in Walker's life. The essay begins with Walker's first memories of herself as a cute two-and-a-half-year-old. The essay calls forth a moment on Easter Sunday 1950 when she is six years old and has just flawlessly delivered an Easter speech in front of all the members of her church. "Isn't she the *cutest* thing!" is included in the compliments that Walker remembers people saying about her, and then she writes, "It was great fun being cute. But then, one day, it ended."[36] Retelling the details of how the eye "accident" took place at the age of eight, Walker gives a moment-by-moment account of how her brother "accidentally" shot her in the eye with a BB gun. Following the account, the essay breaks to a memory of a conversation that Walker shared had with her mother and sister as an adult, about how she changed after the accident. The "midlife crisis" flash returns to Walker as eight years old again, at school, after the accident. "At my old school there is at least one teacher who loves me...it is she who makes life bearable. It is her presence that finally helps me turn on the one child at the school who continually calls me 'one-eyed bitch.' One day I simply grab him by his coat and beat him until I am satisfied."[37] The essay continues with another memory in which Walker remembers sitting beside her mother, deathly ill in bed, and recalling the pain of having to be sent away from her family in Milledgeville to live with her grandparents. A quick turn returns the reader to the adult conversation Walker has with her mother and sister regarding their recollection of whether Walker changed after the "accident." "'You did not change,' they say."[38]

At age twelve Walker recalls abusing her eye almost nightly, yelling at it in the mirror and praying each day for beauty. Next, the essay flashes to a scene of Walker at age fourteen, with her older brother Bill. The two are at a local hospital in Boston where Dr. Morris M. Henry removes the "glob" (the extracapsular cataract) from her eye.[39] She writes about the first moments after the surgery, saying,

> There is still a small bluish crater where the scar tissue was, but the ugly white stuff is gone. Almost immediately I become a different person from the girl who does not raise her head. Or so I think. Now that I've raised my head I win the boyfriend of my dreams. Now that I've raised my head I have plenty of friends. Now that I've raised my head classwork comes from my lips as faultlessly as Easter speeches did, and I leave high school as valedictorian.[40]

Finally, the essay flashes to four incidents of her adulthood. The first recalls a moment in 1984, when she confronts again her insecurities related to her eye. On the night before a magazine shoot, during which a photographer is scheduled to take "glamorous" pictures of her, she fears that her eye will not be "straight enough" for the cover picture on the magazine featuring articles on her latest book. Then, with the help of her lover, she reminds herself that she has "made peace" with her eye already.

The second flashback toward the end of the essay recalls a moment when Walker is talking with her brother Jimmy, who remembers how Walker's father tried to hail a car from the side of the road for help the day Walker was shot. "All I remember is standing by the side of the highway with Daddy, trying to flag down a car. A white man stopped, but when Daddy said he needed somebody to take his little girl to the doctor, he drove off."[41]

The third flash of Walker's adult life shows an image of Walker at age twenty-five, seeing the desert for the first time. Remembering the cruel words of the first doctor her parents brought her to after the accident, "Eyes are sympathetic. If one is blind, the other will likely become blind too,"[42] she recalls bowing down in gratitude for being able to see the beauty of the desert and for the poems that flowed out of that experience.

Finally, the essay flashes to Walker at age twenty-seven as she is putting her three-year-old daughter down for a nap. It is Rebecca who is able to help Walker reclaim herself and reidentify with the wound that has caused her so much physical and emotional pain. In a moment of youthful inquiry, Rebecca, reminded of a children's program in which the world first appears like a "Big Blue Marble," points out the likeness of the cartoon world to her mother's eye. "Mommy, there's a world in your eye.... Mommy, where did you get the world in your eye?"[43] Rebecca's natural embrace of her mother's unique feature helps Walker to embrace herself in a new way. "Crying and laughing I ran to the bathroom.... Yes indeed, I realized, looking into the mirror. There was a world in my eye. And I saw that it was possible to love it: that in fact, for all it had taught me of shame and anger and inner vision, I did love it."[44]

Early Activist and College Years

Self-Love and Racial Awareness

Alice Walker's ability to love herself regardless of her eye injury and the racist and dehumanizing treatment she encountered, as a young black woman growing up in the South, would later become significant themes in her nonfiction and fiction work.[45] According to Walker, self-love was one of the only fully humanizing and spiritually empowering tools strong enough to eradicate the systemic self-hatred fed to blacks over centuries of physical, emotional, and psychological slavery. One way in which hatred of blacks was transported into the American psyche (and self-hatred was projected into the minds of black people) when Walker was growing up was through images of blacks in passive, unintelligent servant roles on primetime television. In some cases, blacks were not shown on television programs at all. Walker writes about the negative impact *not* seeing blacks on TV (and seeing blacks in solely servant roles) had on her mother, who enjoyed watching soap operas during a break from her hard work. In the nonfiction essay "The Civil Rights Movement: What Good Was It?" Walker implies that, like her mother, black people often interpreted the lack of black presence in the media as a message of self-hatred. This critique of the media uncovers a connection between the unethical decisions made by television producers and directors who favored white only TV shows, white actors, and only selected racially biased images so as to prompt any viewer to react negatively toward black peoples or other peoples of color. Walker suggests that this racially biased use of media was interpreted by black folks, as purporting a message of self-hatred. After watching the white characters on the soap operas, who symbolized a racially superior and fantasy-like life, her mother's reaction was always the same. "She would sigh and go out to the kitchen looking lost and unsure of herself."[46] Writing further about how the media images shook her mother's self-image and self-assurance, Walker explains that the images made her mother feel like "she did not exist compared to 'them' [white people].... She could not even bring herself to blame 'them' for making her believe what they wanted her to believe: that if she did not look like them, think like them...she was a nobody."[47]

According to Walker, self-love and empowerment had to be used to destroy the "silent killer" of black self-esteem.. In 1960, it was precisely that image of self-love and empowerment that Walker remembers seeing on TV as she watched Dr. Martin Luther King Jr., arrested in Alabama. Immediately, Walker's life of activism took shape.

> Like a good omen for the future, the face of Dr. Martin Luther King,
> Jr., was the first black face I saw on our new television screen. And,
> as in the fairy tale, my soul was stirred by the meaning for me of his

mission—at the time he was being rather ignominiously dumped in to a police van for having led a protest march in Alabama—and I fell in love with the sober and determined face of the Movement.[48]

Early Activism

Alice Walker joined the civil rights movement as an activist at the age of sixteen. Moved by the passionate dedication and nonviolent action of King and convinced by the fact that her own experience of racism (and that of the many she knew and loved) could not be overlooked, Walker joined the movement with the desire to understand the complexities of racial injustice and to take a stand against it.

Even as a teen, Walker's bold stance against racist behavior made her a "force" to be reckoned with in her community. Recalling Walker's deep sentiments about justice, her high school boyfriend, Porter Sanford III, and another friend, Bobby "Tug" Baines, said that Walker "never accepted the lowly station of blacks in the South. She was conscious of the injustices long before the rest of us recognized them and started to fight."[49] By the time she was a junior in high school, Walker was already well aware of the impact the 1954 *Brown v. Board of Education* desegregation case had on American education and well informed about the actions and strategies of the sit-in movement and boycotts, including the Montgomery Bus Boycott in 1955. Yet, merely witnessing the beginning of change was not enough for Alice Walker; she wanted to be a part of it. Describing the origins of her activism in the movement early in life, she writes,

> As a poet and writer...activism is often my muse...it is organic. Grounded in my mother's love of beauty, the well-tended garden and the carefully swept yard...and in my father's insistence, even as a poor black man...that black people deserved the vote, [and] black children deserved decent schools.[50]

Sitting back and not protesting racial injustice was not an option for Walker; but her decision to join the movement would not be altogether easy. Just as America was undergoing a major social transformation, her life was also undergoing a change. In 1961, Walker would graduate from high school and move into college. Having dedicated herself to the movement, she would have to learn to balance a life of activism with a life of studies at one of the most prestigious Southern schools for black women—Spelman College. In the fall of 1961, she left her home in Eatonton, Georgia, with the hope of becoming a writer and an activist. Only time would confirm that she could be both.

Spelman College

Armed with a mind open to learning, a typewriter, a new suitcase, and a sewing machine (gifts from her mother), Walker prepared to leave for college with seventy-five dollars in her pocket—a gift from friends, family, teachers, and well-wishers from the community. Her father drove her from her home in Eatonton to the Greyhound bus that would carry her into Atlanta. In a final act of protest before she left home, Walker boarded the segregated bus and purposely sat in the front section marked "reserved" for white passengers. She was forced to leave her seat when a white woman complained to the bus driver that by the laws of segregation no black woman had the right to sit where any white person wanted to. But even as she moved "in confusion and tears," Walker recalls, "everything changed. I was eager to bring an end to the South that permitted my humiliation."[51]

Spelman College, an institution of higher learning for black women, was founded on April 11, 1881.[52] In 1961, Alice Walker would be one of the few students admitted on scholarship to the school, but one of many students who became influenced by Spelman's strict rules, religious convictions, and practical *high society* training. By the time Walker entered Spelman, the school had an eighty-year history of educating, nurturing, cultivating black women of "gentility" and providing practical and moral skills that were supposed to guide them on their paths toward becoming a part of the Negro social elite, in and outside of Atlanta. Even though Spelman had a focus on intellectual development and academic preparation in 1961, the school still held onto very "old fashioned" traditions that arguably hindered learning.

In his book *You Can't Be Neutral on a Moving Train,* one-time Spelman College professor Howard Zinn (Walker's favorite professor) describes the school during the 1960s and the pressure placed on students to perform in traditional feminine ways.

> [Students] were expected to dress a certain way, walk a certain way, pour tea a certain way. There was a compulsory chapel six times a week. Students had to sign in and out of their dormitories, and be in

by 10:00 pm. Their contacts with men were carefully monitored; the college authorities were determined to counter stories of the sexually free black woman and worse, the pregnant, unmarried black girl.... It was as if there was an unwritten, unspoken agreement between the white power structure of Atlanta and the administration of the black colleges: We white folk will let you colored folk have your nice little college.... And in return, you will not interfere with our way of life.[53]

Certainly, all these rules, plus the pressure of producing top-notch work, meant that protesting racial injustice in Atlanta streets was not considered a good use of a Spelman student's time by the administration. Still, anxious to be a part of the movement, Walker divided her time between civil rights rallies and school work; during her freshman and sophomore years, she excelled in classes, including elementary French, English composition, Russian history, and ballet. But in 1963, a simple change at Spelman would convince Walker that it was no longer the place for her to continue her education.

In the summer of 1963, Spelman College President Albert Manley fired Howard Zinn, a tenured professor of History. Zinn had been Walker's favorite professor because of his personal commitment to the movement and his special encouragement of her work as a writer. "He was funny, friendly, and genuinely...respected my intelligence," Walker remembers.[54] The dismissal of Zinn came as a great shock to Walker, who, along with her peers, prepared to start a letter-writing campaign to protest his dismissal. In subsequent letters to her beloved professor, Walker tried to express her deep disappointment in the school and her deep support of him. "I've tried to imagine Spelman without you—and I can't at all.... You know how much you mean to us. Whatever I can do to help please *please* let me know."[55]

Another event that caused Walker to rethink the education she was receiving at Spelman was the March on Washington that took place in Washington, DC, on August 28, 1963. Experiencing Martin Luther King Jr.'s "I Have a Dream" speech and witnessing the need for young civil rights workers like herself to become more involved, Walker returned to Atlanta more focused on gaining the education that the movement could give her than the education Spelman could offer. In the fall of her junior year, she wrote another letter to Zinn describing her unfulfilled life at Spelman. "There is nothing really here for me—it is almost like being buried alive. It seems almost a matter of getting away or losing myself—my self—in this strange, unreal place."[56] Following her heart and with the support of her boyfriend, David DeMoss, Alice Walker withdrew from Spelman College in December of 1963. She would return again decades later to address the 1995 Spelman College graduating class, recalling her years since being a Spelman student and presenting her own poetry as graduation gifts.

> My years since leaving Spelman have been rich in experiences of all kinds: in creativity, in struggle, in suffering, in growth, in evolution and change. The poet in me has made good use of everything, and as I look back, the poems are like glistening stones along the moist riverbank of trial and error I have walked along...it is the essence, the poem of my experience, that you deserve as medicine for your own journeys.[57]

Sarah Lawrence College

> When I came to Sarah Lawrence in 1964, I was fleeing from Spelman College in Atlanta, a school that I considered opposed to change, to freedom, and to understanding that by the time most girls enter college they are already women and should be treated as women.[58]

When Walker left Spelman in 1963, she left behind a very visible paper trail. Having been outraged by Zinn's dismissal, Walker published a very strongly worded and brilliantly constructed protest letter in the Spelman College student newspaper, the *Spotlight*.[59] Many took note of Walker's bold stance against the administration, but unique among them was history professor Staughton Lynd. His mother, Helen Merrell Lynd, was a long-standing and well-respected professor at Sarah Lawrence College in Bronxville, New York. A school that linked education to the "experiences, interests and capacities of the individual student,"[60] the New York school, Staughton Lynd thought, might be just the place where Walker's writing talent and commitment to the civil rights movement might be appreciated. His mother agreed.

In 1964, Walker's high academic scores sealed her academic transfer to Sarah Lawrence College. When she informed her parents of her move, Walker's sister, Annie Ruth, remembers, "My parents were very supportive of her. They figured she knew what was best."[61] Walker recalls her experience of adapting to the new environment and her trouble adopting the new styles and ways of Sarah Lawrence.

> In the process of getting adequate clothes, books, and all the other things I didn't have, coming from Georgia, it was really strange for me to see so many women from wealthy families...dressed in rags. It took me a while to understand this aesthetic of the rags and "dressing down" because *my* struggle had been not to wear rags.[62]

The great disparity between experiences of those with wealth and experiences of those born into poverty would become daily reminders to Walker as she made her way through Sarah Lawrence. At the same time, it was her experience, the values she held, and her perspective as a young black woman raised poor and in the South that made her literary voice unique at the college. There was a lot to get used to, but the freedom of expression that Walker experienced through her course work at Sarah Lawrence, the quality attention teachers gave to her writing, and the right she felt she had to fully participate in the movement while being a student made Walker's experience at Sarah Lawrence an exceptional one. Compared to the classrooms at Spelman College, the experience at Sarah Lawrence would help prepare her with the well-rounded education she would need to start a writing career.

Working to Write Well

"She wrote with a daring and force that separated her from the rest"[63] is how one professor, Jane Cooper, described Walker's short story "The Suicide of an American Girl." Walker submitted the story as part of her senior-level course work, but it caught the attention of the entire literary community. Though humbled by this honorable mention, Walker was convinced that her talent was not limited to writing just short stories and essays; Walker also explored other genres of interest. Poetry would become one of Walker's favorite literary genres. In years to come, readers would consider her poems masterpieces through which she could express the deepest of emotions in the clearest of tones. Indeed, it was poetry that would best serve Walker during one of the hardest phases of her life.[64]

In the summer of 1965, Walker was awarded two opportunities to fill her time away from course work. The first was to return to the South as a civil rights worker in Liberty County, Georgia, to register voters in spite of the angry whites and guaranteed police brutality. The second was to join a Vermont-based foreign study group and travel to Africa. Walker chose to go South. "As those rocks and bottles whizzed past my head, I realized I could easily lose the sight in my other eye...there was no support for us in the community and I wasn't ready to be a martyr just then. I had a fall back position, so I quit."[65] Walker returned to New York in time to join the traveling group on their way to Kenya.

It was the deep admiration of compassion and care expressed by the people of Uganda, that drew Walker to Africa. Walker had witnessed some of this depth of caring through her Spelman College roommate, Constance Nabwire whom she kept in touch with while at Sarah Lawrence College. However, the depths of poverty and impact of colonialism made Walker's pilgrimage there hard to endure. A visit from an old friend would completely transform Walker's experience in Africa. David DeMoss, Walker's former boyfriend, was working in Tanzania with the Peace Corps and decided to surprise Walker. The old lovers rekindled their flame, and as Walker retells the story, "we had sex.... I knew immediately that I was pregnant."[66]

As White's biography makes clear, Walker's decision to have an abortion was not really her own. Even after notifying David DeMoss that he was the father, the federal government implanted itself in her way. In 1965, abortion was illegal in the United States. The *Roe v. Wade Supreme Court* case that legalized abortion was eight years away; and being relatively new to New York, Walker's student and economic status, combined with her race, meant that she had no major resources to get "undocumented" medical help on her own. As the pregnancy began to take shape, and the nausea set in, Walker's sense of hopelessness became overwhelming.

> I felt at the mercy of everything, including my own body...I was so sick I could not even bear the smell of fresh air. And I had no money, and I was, essentially—as I had been since grade school—alone. I felt there was no way out...I planned to kill myself...I thought of my mother, to whom abortion is a sin;...my father...who had not helped me at all since I was twelve years old.... my sisters...
>
> I had wasted so much, how dared I?...For three days I lay on the bed with a razor blade under my pillow...I practiced a slicing motion. So that when there was no longer any hope, I would be able to cut my wrists quickly.[67]

As recounted in the interviews of Walker's friends, a few of them worked feverishly to find the contact number of a doctor who would perform an abortion. "Just as Alice had made peace with her decision [suicide], another classmate, Brooke Newman, found a doctor on the Upper East Side of Manhattan who performed abortions. His fee?

An otherworldly $2,000 cash."[68] Diana Young, David DeMoss, and Carole Darden, along with a few other classmates, pieced together the money just in time. Walker recalls the moment, in an article from *In Search of Our Mothers' Gardens,* writing about the day she went in to have the procedure: "I went to see the doctor and he put me to sleep. When I woke up, my friend was standing over me holding a red rose.... she said nothing as she handed me back my life....She drove me back to school and tucked me in. My other friend...brought me food."[69]

The experience, the trauma, and the stress that mounted up to the moment of the abortion would erupt out of Walker onto the page. In less than one week, she would write more than twenty poems. The collection would eventually become Walker's first published work, *Once.*[70] She was twenty-one.

Three years of college life, a graduation, two marriage proposals (one she declined from Julius Coles and one she offered to Mel Leventhal), and several jobs later, Walker would remember the birthing pains of the poems in *Once* almost matter-of-factly.

By the time *Once* was published, it no longer seemed important—I was surprised when it went, almost immediately, into a second printing— that is, the book itself did not seem to me important; only the writing of the poems, which clarified for me how very much I loved being alive.[71]

Her love of life would eventually persuade Walker to move into the Deep South and make significant contributions to the civil rights movement as a writer, journalist, and teacher. But her first move southward would land her on the Lower East Side of Manhattan.

The Activist, Mothering, and Professional Writing Years

Starting Again

Immediately after graduation from Sarah Lawrence in 1966, Walker worked as a caseworker for the New York welfare department for six months. Witnessing the poor care New York hospitals gave to welfare patients, Walker became convinced that the city and federal government needed to take a more radical approach and change domestic health care policy. She joined marches protesting the government's domestic policies as well as its foreign policies that were feeding the ongoing war in Vietnam. Just as protests for racial equality had been a crucial part of Walker's life in Atlanta, hitting the New York streets in protest for the fullness of humanity and proper treatment of all persons, including the Vietnamese, became a routine part of Walker's life in the North.

Overwhelmed and burnt out from "trying to personally save the walking wounded," Walker quit her caseworker job and tried to begin her life as a writer.[72] A fellowship, offered to her at Spelman, which she turned down at the time, was reoffered to her by Charles Merrill for the summer of 1966. Walker originally planned to use the two thousand dollars to travel to Senegal and study French, but at the last minute she changed her mind.

Mississippi was one of the most dangerous states in which to participate in the civil rights movement. Racist mobs of angry white people were known to become violent, and the state police did little to help black or white civilians in the movement to escape the brutality with their lives. The overwhelming fear and constant brutality also made Mississippi one of the Southern states most in need of movement workers who were willing to establish voter registration campaigns and spread the word about racial equality. After securing a job with the NAACP Legal Defense and Educational Fund, Walker opted out of her chance to become more educated in French and decided instead to head straight into the heart of Mississippi. It was there that she would meet the dangers, transformations, and hidden complexities of the movement head on.

Activism, Motherhood, and the Movement

Upon arriving in Mississippi in the summer of 1966, Walker was greeted by a movement worker from the NAACP Legal Defense Fund (LDF) office led by Marian Wright (later, Marian Wright Edelman). The two went to lunch to discuss some of the work Walker would be doing. At the restaurant, Walker met Melvyn Leventhal for the first time. "I remember thinking he was cute," Walker later recalled.[73] Leventhal was a twenty-three-year-old New York University Law School student who worked with the Law Students' Civil Rights Research Council in Jackson during the previous summer. In 1966, he returned to Jackson to work directly for Marian Wright with the NAACP LDF. Leventhal could easily be spotted among other civil rights legal aids and workers. He was young, Jewish, and quite innocent of the deep racism of the South. Years later he would remark upon his courage to get involved with the movement, saying, "If I had ever studied up on exactly how dangerous it was to try to end segregation in Mississippi, I might not have had the courage to go.... My ignorance is what saved me."[74]

Since they were working for the same office, Walker and Leventhal would find themselves working together quite often. This was the case when the two were assigned to take depositions and record the stories from sharecroppers treated unfairly in Greenwood, Mississippi. Walker and Leventhal traveled from Jackson together by car, and Leventhal assumed that they would be able to rest as soon as they checked into their hotel rooms. Regardless of the changes that had been made in the courtrooms in Washington, DC, the traditional "Ole Boys' Mississippi" segregation law was still firmly in place in Greenwood. Upon their arrival at the hotel, the clerk refused to give Walker a room. Recalling how much Leventhal's naïveté angered her, she remembers the moment, saying, "Mel was shaking his head in disbelief and saying, 'I can't believe they don't want to let you stay here,' and other remarks that reflected the naïveté that so many Northerners displayed when they came to the South. Did he think that just because some laws had been changed, white people were automatically going to start treating blacks like human beings? That kind of attitude infuriated me."[75]

Angry, but more afraid of the legendary Mississippi "good ole boys" known to ransack movement workers on location, chase them off roads, shoot them dead, and then burn the evidence, Walker and Leventhal mutually decided that they were better off staying together in one hotel room. Too afraid to go to sleep, the two read to each other from the Song of Solomon from the hotel Bible most of the night. Walker would later confess, "Nothing romantic happened that evening, but our souls had touched."[76] One year and countless escapes from Ku Klux Klansmen, ominous police traffic stops, and other dangerous and racist encounters later, Walker and Leventhal were married in New York City on March 17, 1967. They would return south that same year, interracially married, and by their very nature, upsetting to the traditional laws of racism in Mississippi.

Mississippi: Home

Walker and Leventhal made Mississippi their home for seven years. During that time, Leventhal continued working as a civil rights attorney with the NAACP, and Walker worked as a professor at various institutions, including Jackson State College and Tougaloo College. She also worked to develop and teach a curriculum for adult literacy Headstart programs in the South. And, of course, Walker continued her writing. The year 1967 brought fortune to Walker when she won an essay contest from the *American Scholar*. In 1968, her debut poetry collection *Once* was published, and not more than two years later she would finish her first novel, *The Third Life of Grange Copeland*. Over the years, Walker learned to balance her writing and professional career with her life of activism, but being illegally interracially married to Leventhal brought tremendous stress upon her and their marriage. Leventhal's relatively high profile as a civil rights attorney during the peak of the movement also made living *safely* in Mississippi difficult. Both Walker and Leventhal agreed with King's nonviolent philosophy; however, the couple also believed in protecting their rights and their liberty by any means necessary. Leventhal kept a loaded weapon in his car and in their home to use in the case of an emergency.

While their careers were both moving forward, Walker would later recall how stagnant and suffocated she felt in Mississippi. In her essay "Recording the Seasons," she remembers how suicidal she felt while living in the deeply racist state. "I grew to adulthood in Mississippi. And yet, the cost was not minor. Always a rather moody, periodically depressed person, after two years in Mississippi I became—as I had occasionally been as a young adult—suicidal."[77] In addition to the stress of movement work and pursuing her own writing deadlines, Walker and Leventhal were faced with the dilemma of whether to have a child.

"Curiosity. Boredom. Avoiding the Draft" are three reasons that Walker admits to thinking through when she and Leventhal decided to have a child.[78] In her essay "One Child of One's Own: A Meaningful Digression within the Work(s)," Walker recounts that just as the government had had a hand in her decision to have an abortion years before, the government also had a hand in her decision to give birth. Her own curiosity about motherhood and the boredom she felt between writing projects were major reasons to take into consideration, but the looming threat that influenced her decision to bear a child was that her husband Leventhal might be sent to prison for objecting to fight in the Vietnam War if he could not prove that he was a "family man." This became an important part of the decision for Walker to get pregnant.[79]

By early 1968, Walker was pregnant, but hearing the news of Martin Luther King Jr.'s assassination on April 4, 1968, would take all the life out of her. She recalls in her essay "Coretta King: Revisited" the dark moment she felt in her heart and womb.

> When I saw Coretta again it was at Dr. King's funeral, when my husband and I marched behind her husband's body in anger and despair....In my heart I said good-bye to the nonviolence she still professed. I was far less calm than she appeared to be. The week after that long, four mile walk across Atlanta, and after the tears and anger and the feeling of turning gradually to stone, I lost the child I had been carrying. I did not even care. It seemed to me, at the time, that if "he" (it was weeks before my tongue could form his name) must die no one deserved to live, not even my own child.[80]

After some time, Walker and Leventhal would try to get pregnant again. They were successful; and on November 17, 1969, Rebecca Grant Leventhal was born, three days after Walker finished writing her second book. Ten years later, Walker would recall her experience of giving birth and share her fears and reflections on being a mother.

> It is perfectly true that I, like many other women who work, especially as writers, was terrified of having children. I feared being fractured by the experience if not overwhelmed. I thought the quality of my writing would be considerably diminished by motherhood—that nothing that was good for my writing could come out of having children.... My first mistake was in thinking "children" instead of "child." My second was in seeing The Child as my enemy rather than the racism and sexism of a capitalist society.[81]

Of her experience of giving birth, she would write,

> What is true about giving birth is...that it is miraculous.... For one thing, though my stomach was huge and the baby (?!) constantly causing turbulence within it, I did not believe a baby, a person, would come out of me. I mean, look what had gone in....The point was, I was changed forever. From a woman whose "womb" had been, in a sense, her head—that is to say, certain small seeds had gone in, and rather different if not larger or better "creations" had come out—to a woman who...had two wombs![82]

Working and writing from two wombs would change not only Walker's writing career but also her writing style and life. In 1970, she received the news that her first novel (*The Third Life of Grange Copeland*) was published; she also came to know that she was awarded the Radcliffe Institute Fellowship Award. The fellowship offered her a break from her stressful life in Mississippi; and even though it meant moving her daughter and herself to Cambridge away from her husband for a year, Walker accepted the opportunity. In September of 1971, Walker was settled in a new apartment and ready to begin research. A harsh winter and a terrible flu virus welcomed both Walker and Rebecca to the East Coast. They survived, and in the spring, Walker was approached about teaching a course at Wellesley College. "Within the first few meetings, it was clear this was going to be my most important course in college," one of Walker's former students in the class remarked.[83]

Having thoroughly impressed the faculty at Wellesley and the surrounding scholarly community, Walker became extremely involved as a teacher and pushed back her deadline for her novel *Meridian*. She needed more time. So, in 1972, she wrote to the Radcliffe Institute and requested an additional year of funding. Her request was granted, but it wasn't the only decision Walker would have to make. Her baby daughter's recurring illnesses brought home the reality that Rebecca needed to be raised in a warmer climate. Faced with a hard choice, Walker and Leventhal decided it was best to send their baby back to Jackson for the sake of her health. Rebecca arrived safely back in Jackson with her father, and Walker joined her just a month later. Walker traveled back and forth from Cambridge to Jackson returning in the spring and staying with Rebecca and her husband through the fall. Though Walker was never away from Rebecca for more than a month, it began to be clear that the commuting was taking a toll. That year, Walker recalls taking Rebecca with her when she left Mississippi and enrolling her in the Radcliffe Day care. While nothing was made official at the time, Walker and Leventhal's marriage lay in the balance. "The situation was hard on both of us," Leventhal would later say.[84]

During her time in Cambridge, Walker would finish two of her most important early works. Some of the poems in *Revolutionary Petunias & Other Poems* were fueled by Walker's struggle to maintain a strained marriage and her sadness at being away from her daughter. Some of the stories of her family's past, her own experiences, and the experiences of other black women she had met during her work in the movement would fuel the imagination for stories in *In Love & Trouble: Stories of Black Women*.[85] At the end of the

1972–1973 school year and after having spent two years away from her home in Mississippi, Walker returned to the Southern state. That same year she would experience the death of her father and uncover the unmarked gravesite of Zora Neale Hurston. Walker writes explicitly about the impact of her father's death in her essay "Father" in her book *Living by the Word*. Walker's essays recording her quest to find Zora Neale Huston are two of her most renowned "Looking for Zora" and "Zora Neale Hurston: A Cautionary Tale and a Partisan View," are both found in her book *In Search of Our Mothers' Gardens*. After experiencing the freedom of the North, Walker could not stay in Mississippi; and so, according to her (then) husband's recollection, she said, " 'Mel, it's our marriage or Mississippi. You've got to make up your mind.' Since the marriage was more important, we packed up and left."[86]

In Her Own Words

New York City became Alice, Mel, and Rebecca's new home; and while Leventhal worked as a civil rights attorney for the NAACP Legal Defense and Educational Fund office in New York, Walker's previous work, *In Love & Trouble,* was already making a way for her to work with a new genre of writing. Walker's short story "Roselily," from that collection, had been published in *Ms. Magazine* in August 1972. So by the time Walker arrived in New York City, the magazine's cofounder, Gloria Steinem, was ready to offer Walker a job. In 1974, Walker became a contributing editor of *Ms. Magazine*; and while other magazines certainly had interest in hiring Walker (including *Essence* magazine), none seemed to fit Walker's style or sociopolitical voice.

Although they tried to keep their marriage together, the demands of Leventhal's job, the shifting atmosphere of the movement as it became more militant and Black Nationalist, and Walker's desire to continue her career with *Ms. Magazine* resulted in Walker and Leventhal's divorce in 1976. The two carefully planned to have joint custody of Rebecca. In the first year, Walker moved across the park from the common house so that Rebecca had two places to choose from. To honor Rebecca's sense of place, in the midst of the shifting, her parents chose to keep her in the same school. Later, when Walker moved to San Francisco, and Leventhal to DC they tried a different approach whereby Rebecca could stay with her mother for two years in San Francisco and two years with her father in Washington, DC.

The plan didn't last long and eventually Rebecca made a choice to attend Urban, a private school in San Francisco and live with her mother.[87] Even in the midst of many life changes, Walker's second novel, *Meridian,* was published.

In 1978, Walker moved to San Francisco after becoming reacquainted with an old friend from Morehouse College, Robert Allen. The two found a home together in Boonville, California, where Walker continued working on her third novel as a collection of poetry; *Goodnight, Willie Lee, I'll See You in the Morning* published in 1979. A collection of autobiography, articles, essays, and work by Zora Neale Hurston, *I Love Myself When I Am Laughing...and Then Again When I Am Looking Mean and Impressive* was also published in this year. In 1981, Walker's *You Can't Keep a Good Woman Down,* including fourteen stories of how black women have survived, was published.

The years 1982 and 1983 brought a whirlwind of success to Walker's life and career as she finished her third novel, *The Color Purple.* The book is an epistolary novel that evokes the theme of self-love through the life story of Celie. As previously noted, the storyline of the book was taken from an experience that Walker's sister, Annie Ruth, witnessed as a child. Young, female, and poor, Celie is a black girl living during the early 1900s in a sharecropper family under the oppressive conditions of racism, sexism, and poverty. In the book, Celie starts to express herself at the age of forteen, through letters that she has written to God about the pain of being repeatedly raped by a man she thinks is her father. Having been impregnated and forced to give her children away, Celie becomes fearful that her sister Nettie will endure the same fate. Celie urges her sister to go and work for a nearby missionary family, to whom her own children have been sent. Nettie is freed, but Celie, no longer considered "acceptable" to her stepfather's advances, is forced into an abusive marriage to Mr. ____ and mandated to care for his and his children's needs. Having no recourse or power to protect herself, Celie is pushed into abusive, slave-like conditions while carrying the additional weight of societal oppressions and feeling a deep isolation from her sister.

Celie finds a new sisterhood in the most unlikely person of Shug Avery, a juke-joint singer and on-again-off-again lover of Mr.____'s. Shug's occasional visits eventually merge into a protective sisterhood and loving relationship for Celie. With Shug's help, Celie is able to avoid the normal dose of abusive treatment given by her husband and experience love for herself with Shug. Toward the end of the book, Celie finds the courage to love herself, regardless of her past, and be an independent, thinking black woman. In *The Color Purple,* Celie overcomes a multitude of oppressions constructed to destroy her soul and proves the power of the human spirit to rise above impossibilities and love herself regardless.

The universality of the book and the powerful themes of humanity, love, and women's experiences of living into wholeness made *The Color Purple* an overnight success. Just a year after it was published, *The Color Purple* was awarded the Pulitzer Prize in fiction and its author Walker named as the first black woman to receive the high honor.

In less than three years, the book was released as a film (December 1985) directed by Stephen Spielberg and scored by Quincy Jones. In February of 1986, the film was nominated for eleven Oscar awards. Though it did not win even one award, the movie was a success in Walker's eyes because her mother, Minnie Lou, at the age of seventy-four, "took pride in all of Walker's achievements, but the movie was extra special because she could relate to the characters personally."[88]

Building upon the theme of self-love explored in *The Color Purple,* Walker would write another collection of nonfiction essays, published in 1983, that would have earthshaking consequences for black women in all kinds of communities, including the academy. *In Search of Our Mothers' Gardens: A Womanist Prose* would become another one of Walker's signature pieces. This collection of essays, journal entries, articles, and book reviews records Walker's own ethical thoughts and reflections upon the civil rights movement, the importance of activism and revolution, being a Southern black writer, and being a black woman.

The theme of self-love is highlighted repeatedly in Walker's nonfiction works, and is especially noted in her definition of the term "womanist." The third part of the definition of womanist most adequately focuses on the theme of self-love, reflecting on black women's connection between the self and the community. At the time of writing it, the term "womanist" had specific meaning for Walker in that it gave black women who identified with the feminist movement a chance to name themselves differently from how white feminists named black feminists. It also allowed black women to present their own experiences of racism, classism, and sexism as important aspects of analysis when looking at social, political, racial, and economic issues. In her essay "Audre's Voice," Walker describes in detail what she meant by the term "womanist." She recalls a conversation with black feminist Audre Lorde and explains the distinction between womanist and black feminist to Lorde, who believed *womanist* was designed to cause a rift within black feminism.

> She had questioned my use of the word "womanist," in lieu of "black feminist," saying that it appeared to be an attempt to disclaim being feminist...I pointed out to her that it is a necessary act of liberation to name oneself with words that fit; that this was a position her own work celebrated.... We talked until Audre seemed to understand my point about using the word "womanist": more room in it for changes, said I, sexual and otherwise. More reflective of black women's culture, especially Southern culture.[89]

The meaning of the term and the capacity to express black women's experience with "more room in it for changes" than the term "feminist" gave rise to a new black women's consciousness that was "devoid of the damning social stigmas affiliated with women's liberation."[90] The term also surfaced as an essential title for black women in the field of religion, who were attempting to expand the discourse of religious experience to include black women's experiences and viewpoints of (Christian) religion. Such forerunners of this movement included Katie G. Cannon, Delores S. Williams, and Jacquelyn Grant. The key to what eventually would be named the new religious discourse, "Womanist Theology," was making black women's experiences central to the telling and shaping of a theological lens. It was not only Walker's coinage of the term that gave these scholars gumption to write but also her fiction and nonfiction that supported them to give themselves permission to place black women at the center of discourse, which otherwise considered Eurocentric viewpoints dominant and valid. Placing black women's experiences at the center and uncovering their stories were central themes in Walker's definition of "womanist."

As the limelight and the controversies sparked by *The Color Purple* began to fade (the film was considered controversial because of its portrayal of violence in black families, abuse at the hands of black men, and its embrace of a lesbian relationship between black women), Walker turned her attention to publishing. In 1984, she launched a small publishing firm, Wild Tree Press, with partner Robert Allen and friend Belvie Rooks. She gave attention to and nurtured the work of new writers and continued writing herself. The end of 1984 brought the publication of Walker's twelfth book, a collection of poetry, *Horses Make a Landscape Look More Beautiful*. Throughout filming, production, and release of the movie *The Color Purple*, Walker continued writing essays about her own life experience and capturing the experience of others through fiction and nonfiction work. In 1988, her work emerged in the form of two books, *To Hell with Dying* and *Living by the Word*. *The Temple of My Familiar*, published in 1989, was one of her most anticipated novels because it followed the life of Celie from her coming of age and coming to voice debuted in *The Color Purple*. *The Temple of My Familiar* was published after seven years of writing the Pulitzer Prize–winning book, and this new book received both good and bad reviews. Walker was not deterred. Just as she had done when she had been confronted by controversies and critiques before, she kept writing. Beginning in 1991, Walker published at least one book of poetry, nonfiction book, or novel a year for more than ten years (except for the years 1995, 1999, and 2002), and she is still writing. Her works, from that period, include

1991—*Finding the Green Stone and Her Blue Body Everything We Know*
1992—*Possessing the Secret of Joy*
1993—*Warrior Marks*
1994—*Alice Walker: The Complete Stories*
1996—*The Same River Twice*
1997—*Anything We Love Can Be Saved: A Writer's Activism*
1998—*By the Light of My Father's Smile*
2000—*The Way Forward Is with a Broken Heart*
2001—*Sent by Earth: A Message from the Grandmother Spirit after the Bombing of the World Trade Center and the Pentagon*
2003—*Absolute Trust in the Goodness of the Earth and a Poem Traveled Down My Arm*
2004—*Now Is the Time to Open Your Heart*
2006—*We Are the Ones We Have Been Waiting For Inner Light in a Time of Darkness Meditations*[91]

As a world-renowned writer and exceptional literary force, Walker employs a distinct style to uncover black women's stories and her method of writing presents universal connections experienced in the lives of humans and earthlings living in creation. Hailing from a sharecroppers' farm in Georgia, Alice Walker has traveled across the world, discussed public policy with diplomats, served as an educator, a mother, a wife, a partner, a civil rights leader, a human rights and social activist, and a writer. It is her role as a writer that has influenced the world the most—and it is in this muse that she continues to inspire.

Survey of Nonfiction Books for This Analysis

Although Walker is most widely known for her fiction work, she is also a prolific nonfiction essayist. Three of Walker's nonfiction books that will serve as sources from which to glean virtues and values for the construction of a womanist virtue ethic include *In Search of Our Mothers' Gardens: Womanist Prose* (1983), *Living by the Word* (1988), and *Anything We Love Can Be Saved: A Writer's Activism* (1997).

In Search of Our Mothers' Gardens was first published in 1983 and (among other things) contains essays, book reviews, articles, and personal, social, and ethical reflection. The collection encompasses Walker's most extensive reflections on her own early activism in the civil rights movement. Some of the articles that appear in *In Search of Our Mothers' Gardens* were first published elsewhere and then later collected for the book. For example, Walker's first award-winning essay, "The Civil Rights Movement: What Good Was It?" was first published in the *American Scholar* in 1967.[92] Other essays were originally delivered as lectures and speeches at colleges and universities. For example, Walker delivered "A Talk: Convocation"[93] at her alma mater, Sarah Lawrence College, in 1972.

Altogether, *In Search of Our Mothers' Gardens* consists of thirty-four essays, grouped into four sections. Most of the works were written between 1966 and 1982 and formed Walker's eleventh book. It was published during a "high" time in her career soon after she was awarded the Pulitzer Prize for *The Color Purple*. Though the genres of writing are different, a metaphor of twins can be used to explain the common themes found in both *The Color Purple* and *In Search of Our Mothers' Gardens*. The metaphor of twins is how I would explain Walker's style of writing. That is to say, themes that she raises in her fiction work are also found in her nonfiction work and in some cases become points from which she explicates certain values. For example, themes including racism, classism, sexism, heterosexism, and poverty are raised consistently throughout *The Color Purple* and illustrated through the life of the character of Celie. These same themes are also addressed in her nonfiction essays in *In Search of Our Mothers' Gardens* as if to extend the conversation of

Walker's thought from a social activist, cultural critical, and ethical perspective.[94]

Living by the Word, Walker's second collection of nonfiction essays and thirteenth book, consists of essays, journal entries, and letters. It was published in 1988, the same year Walker's short story *To Hell with Dying* was published[95] and one year before her fourth novel, *The Temple of My Familiar*, was published. Here the twins metaphor is helpful in charting a connection between themes Walker raises in her fiction work *The Temple of My Familiar* and the ethical virtues and values that she expresses in her nonfiction work *Living by the Word*. Walker's preface to *Living by the Word* reveals a good summary of the book's quest to heighten environmental and global consciousness. This fact, compared with her use of nature and animal characters in the book *The Temple of My Familiar*, suggests that Walker allows her nonfiction voice to be an extension and explication of the moral values signaled from the themes in her fiction.

In comparison to *In Search of Our Mothers' Gardens*, *Living by the Word* is slightly shorter, consisting of twenty-seven entries. In Walker's words, the text carries an overarching theme of "heightened global consciousness" and addresses such topics as her own Native American heritage, civil rights for Native Americans, humanization, and hair.[96]

Anything We Love Can Be Saved: A Writer's Activism is Walker's third collection of nonfiction essays. It was published in 1997, a year before her fiction work *By the Light of My Father's Smile*.[97] It is Walker's twenty-second book and comprises thirty-four entries including essays, illustrations, letters, film reviews, and speeches. This book is unique in that it captures Walker's reflections on the origins and roots of her life of activism. Explaining that she has been an activist "all of my adult life,"[98] Walker connects her activism to her deep desire to savor nature in Earth and her "delight in human beings."[99] She writes, "My activism—cultural, political, spiritual—is rooted in my love of nature and my delight in human beings.... I believe people exist to be enjoyed, much as a restful or engaging view might be. As the ocean or drifting clouds might be."[100]

The seven sections of *Anything We Love Can Be Saved* arrange writings that address various topics, including sexism within the Christian and Rastafarian religions, female genital mutilation, clarifying the origins and meaning of "womanist," and political reflections on the first series of U.S. attacks on Iraq in the early 1990s.

Select essays from each of Walker's nonfiction collections reveal prevalent themes, virtues, and values in her work. As a way of honoring the tradition of womanist religious thought, and more specifically womanist ethics, I now turn to explaining the origins of the discipline and explicate a womanist ethical method to assist in the work of gleaning Walker's essays for virtues and values helpful for the construction of a womanist virtue ethics.

2

A Path Set before Us: Womanist Virtue Method

In North America, the waves of womanist religious thought begin with the wind-like dancing motion of several women scholars of African descent who are engaged in the discourse of religion, theology, biblical studies, and ethics, and dedicated to creating room for their own voices and the voices of their communities. Moving through the landscape of Anglo-American and European scholars and normative theological constructs that in some cases supported the subordination of women and silenced the religious experiences of peoples of color, scholars such as Katie G. Cannon, Delores S. Williams, Jacquelyn Grant, and Renita J. Weems began looking for language outside of the traditional vocabulary to articulate their own theologies and theological reflections upon experiences of surviving, resisting, and overcoming interrelated oppressions.

These Christian theologians, biblical scholars, and ethicists argued that theological concepts such as sacrifice, servanthood, and unmerited suffering, as well as the moral instructions affiliated with them, were interpreted differently from the accepted norm by African American women and other women of African descent as a result of the slavery, segregation, and multiple systems of oppression they have historically experienced. The development of ethical methods of analysis and the examination of how tripartite (race-class-gender) oppressions impact theo-ethical responses can be found in articles such as Cannon's "The Emergence of Black Feminist Consciousness" and in books including Williams's *Sisters in the Wilderness*, Grant's *White Women's Christ and Black Women's Jesus*, and Weems's *Just a Sister Away*.

In these works, each of the authors uses a black feminist/womanist race-class-gender analysis to interrogate theological concepts and the origins of false assumptions that support the idea that racism is divinely ordained by God. They critique the social systems that reinforce economic imbalance and thus maintain systems of poverty. Finally, they critically assess how sexism functions normatively in ecclesial hierarchies, which results in limited opportunities for women and disembodied visions of right living that do not take into account women's lives and realities.

In addition to honoring the theological ideas and constructs from scholars in the dominant culture, womanist religious thought centers the voices, experiences, theological reflections, and moral systems that come from "ordinary" women of African descent. Such knowledge, from mothers, grandmothers, aunts, sisters, partners, and wives, contributes to a new womanist epistemology—that is, a theory of the nature of knowledge—that debunks myths circulating in the dominant culture about the ability of women of African descent to be moral agents. But what does it mean to act with moral agency—when the dominant culture has infused the discipline of religion with the idea that African Americans and peoples of African descent are less than human? This and other questions are examined by the study of womanist ethics.

Womanist Ethics

Womanist ethics is a religious discipline that examines ethical theories concerning human agency, action, and relationship while at the same time critiquing theological constructions that negate the *wholeness* or full existence of women who deal with the realities of social injustice and multilayered oppressions. Using analytical tools that examine how race, class, gender, sexual identity, and Earth relationship impact individual and communal ethical worldviews and constrict the building of moral communities, womanist ethics contributes a much-needed lens through which to view normative Christian and religious ethics. Womanist ethics accomplishes this by lifting up the voices of the historically silenced and naming their perspectives as valid sources of theo-ethical inquiry. Womanist ethics embodies descriptive analytical approaches, detailing the stories, circumstances, and moral ideas articulated by women of African descent. It is also constructive in that it proposes sets of values and systems of ethics that honor the humanity of all people and fight for the full liberation and justice of women, children, and men of African descent as members of the global human community living in the fullness of Creation.[1]

The various elements of womanist ethics—deconstructive (critique), descriptive, and constructive—constantly interact. The multilayered analysis of womanist ethics is deconstructive because it prioritizes the theological and religious reflections of women, inevitably leading to critiques of dominant forms of ethics that omit their experience. It examines ways in which systems of patriarchy, imbalanced power, and normative ethical codes based on the logic of domination are used to oppress women of African descent and their communities.

Subtle ways of enforcing African American women's absence from discourses on topics such as ethics often lie in unspoken institutional practices. Black feminist theory helps womanist ethics explain how African American women (and men) have been excluded from full participation in the academic production of ethical theory. In *Black Feminist Thought*, Patricia Hill Collins explores the way culture generates and assigns credibility to certain kinds of knowledge (often informed directly by the dominant culture) while discounting knowledge that emerges from communities of color and more specifically from the communities of women of African descent. She argues for an alternative approach that validates knowledge claims from black women and their perspectives in academic discourse. Similar to a claim that Katie Cannon makes regarding Christian social ethics, Collins explains that white males have dominated traditional academic discourse so much that they control the structures of epistemology. That is, white men of the elite control what is and is not considered knowledge. According to this dominant epistemology, black women's voices and, more specifically, black feminist thought are not considered primary knowledge but are rather deemed "subjugated knowledge." Forced to begin from this suppressed place, Collins argues for an alternative epistemology or way of producing and validating knowledge that includes "alternative sites such as music, literature, daily conversations, and everyday behavior as important locations for articulating the core themes of a Black feminist consciousness."[2] The purpose of this alternative epistemology is multidimensional in that it (1) validates black women's knowledge as authoritative; (2) elevates black women's knowledge beyond the "subjected" realm; and (3) simultaneously challenges the dominant epistemology. For Collins, including black women's standpoints as part of what is and is not considered knowledge threatens the entire dominant epistemological system. This forces all scholars to reconsider the racist, classist, and sexist reasons black feminist thought may have been deemed subjugated knowledge in the first place. Instead of using Eurocentric epistemologies and approaches, Collins suggests a new method that allows for black women's complex subjectivity to be expressed, involving three steps: (1) the inclusion of experience and naming it authoritative; (2) paying attention to the use of dialogue in the process of reflection; and (3) seeing the act of coming to voice as resistance. As a threefold method itself—deconstructive, descriptive, and constructive—Collins's entire argument clearly provides a companion line of reasoning for all the tasks of womanist ethics and helps articulate its often counter conventional methods and goals.

In seeking to remedy the omission of African American women's experience and knowledge from traditional ethics, womanist ethics turns to the descriptive task of naming their experience as a source of both moral principles and strategies for resistance and survival. Katie G. Cannon, as discussed in the introduction, undertook this task early in her work by looking to black women's literature. Cannon's method is shaped by a black feminist and womanist lens and, therefore, acknowledges experience as a primary entryway into analysis that takes seriously the brutal and fragmenting effects of racism, classism, sexism, heterosexism, and other forms of oppression on the moral and real lives of women of African descent. In addition, Cannon's method helps to uncover the secret wisdom of how to survive interrelated oppressions and some of the virtues that can aid in this process. According to Cannon, black women's literature is an excellent resource because it mirrors real African American life and uncovers effective values.

> Black women's literary tradition is a source in the study of ethics relative to the Black community, because the development of the Black women's historical and literary legacy is tied up with the origin of Black people in America...Black women's writings have paralleled Black history. As creators of literature these women are not formally historians, sociologists, nor theologians, but the patterns and themes in their writings are reflective of historical facts, sociological realities and religious convictions that lie behind the ethos and ethics of the

Black community. As recorders of the Black experience, Black women writers convey the Black community's consciousness of values which enable them to find meaning.[3]

The constructive task can begin from this work of finding meaning. Yet finding meaning in the African Americans' experiences of oppression ought not to be confused with an acceptance of that oppression. I refer here to the mistaken and grievous assumption that womanist constructive ethical approaches are premised on the existence of oppression, suffering, and evil and, therefore, focused solely on providing strategies of enduring and suffering through multiple oppressions. This is far from the truth. Though womanist ethical responses may attend to the question of why does suffering and evil exist in light of the existence of a benevolent God, or other forms of the theodicy question raised by the circumstances of being forced to live through oppression and injustice, womanism is hardly passive. It does not sit back and let bad things happen. Its approaches are designed to uproot racism, classism, sexism, homophobia, Earth injustice, and other forms of oppression by examining them and dismantling them. Womanist ethical approaches are constructive in that they consistently replant justice, opening avenues by which justice can be served, and create (and re-create) virtues and values that promote justice and optimal strategies for living.[4]

Womanist ethical approaches should be viewed as profound modes of resistance to oppression, and acts of violence, that echo ancestral calls for justice and demand and enact change. They proclaim the importance of justice for African American women and African peoples across the Diaspora. Womanist ethics fully and unapologetically acknowledges that its lens is shaped by the theological perspectives of women of African descent and their experiences of and resistance to racism, classism, sexism, heterosexism, and other forms of oppression.[5]

Womanist Virtue Ethical Method

Within the discourse of womanist ethics, several ethical methods are used to mine the stories of women and girls of African descent in order to lift up the morals and values found therein and center theological constructions of God on the basis of their experiences. Through this work, strategies of survival are revealed for these women and their communities and a link between the values and their faith is found.

One of the methods that reveals this path of moral thought is a womanist virtue method.

To chart ethical virtues, values, and norms conducive to the lives of people and specifically women of African descent and establish moral codes that allow for the survival and promotion of wholeness and well-being for African peoples throughout the globe, Cannon's method of mining virtues and values in the work of black literary artists becomes a primary tool in theological ethics. The method is interdisciplinary in that it connects sociohistorical analysis, methods within Christian feminist social ethics, and black women's literature. Cannon argues that to bring forth virtues and values helpful for living African American life, additional sources that uncover the experiences of women of African descent and their communities—including aural and oral history, sermons, speeches, writings, art, and literature—must be considered valid sources for developing womanist epistemologies.

As Cannon writes in her book *Black Womanist Ethics*, African American women's perspectives on what is right and wrong behavior are significantly influenced by the context of oppression they have lived in. "In the Black community, the aggregate of the qualities which determine desirable ethical values regarding the uprightness of character and soundness of moral conduct must always take into account the circumstances."[6] Noting how the circumstances of racial, gender, and economic oppression have constantly barraged the lives, self-determination, and dignity of African Americans, and African American women in particular, Cannon boldly argues that dominant ethical virtues, such as frugality and industry, assume certain principles of life, such as historical political freedom, and thus develop moral codes for ethical living that simply do not mesh with the lives of African American women or their communities. Any ethical system, moral code, or survival strategy that would help guide the lives of these women and their communities has to be determined and shaped by the moral wisdom that has emerged from within the communities and passed down from one generation to the next as "womanist moral wisdom."[7]

For Cannon and other womanist scholars, prioritizing the theo-ethical perspectives and communal and social actions of African American foremothers has shed necessary "womanist light" on notions of Christian morality and ethics that disrupts the false truth assumed in "the dominant ethical systems [that] implied that the doing of Christian ethics in the Black community was either immoral or amoral."[8] Instead, womanist ethics presents valid sources and proof of African American moral wisdom and viable life-affirming ethical systems for African American women and their communities.[9]

The basic steps of Cannon's virtue method include acknowledging the experiences of African American women and communities by surveying black women's literature, lifting experiential themes from this literature, and then gleaning the ethical implications from these themes to determine a set of norms, virtues, and values that reflect the ethics and moral values of African American women and their communities.[10] Cannon's work reveals a set of virtues and argues that any set of canonical virtues or values that are part of a community are indeed shaped by the cultural context and experiences of that community; her method can be considered a womanist virtue ethical method, revealing an influence of Aristotelian ethics.

According to Eve Browning Cole, the Greek philosopher Aristotle was a primary proponent of ethical pluralism wherein "forms of virtue correspond to gender, social class, and political function."[11] Often contrasting with Platonic and Socratic approaches that signaled that a virtue must be realizable, knowable, and definable, Aristotle's sense of virtue made allowances for difference and paid attention to context. Cannon's thought builds on Aristotle in that she borrows this contextual lens when approaching ethics and uses an inductive virtue ethical approach that examines cultural circumstance when determining what is good and bad and right and wrong.[12] She writes, "African American women's appraisal of what is right or wrong and good and bad develops out of the various coping mechanisms related to the conditions of their own cultural circumstances. In the face of this, black women have justly regarded survival against tyrannical systems of race, sex, and class oppression as a true sphere of moral life."[13] Similar to the way in which Aristotle argues in his *Nichomachean Ethics*[14] that ethics are culturally specific, and analysis of the virtues and values that a particular community adheres to must take into consideration the ethos of a particular community, Cannon argues that African American ethics and sets of virtues that operate within that community can be determined by inductively examining black women's literature to find out about the cultural context and real-life experiences of black peoples.

However, the problematic nature of Aristotle's view on women and women's lack of virtue is not lost on Cannon. Highly dualistic in its frame, Aristotle's ethics as well as his view that women by nature have less capacity to be as virtuous as men makes his thought almost antithetical to womanist religious thought. For example, Aristotle's works *Nichomachean Ethics* and *Eudemian Ethics* imply that there is little importance in discussing women's virtue. In fact, the subject is not deeply engaged in either of these monumental texts, but rather in *Rhetoric* wherein Aristotle summarizes women's virtue as being wrapped up in their beauty and their ability to "delight in hard work" and (as is the case with men of Greek culture) to be self-controlled.[15]

Though helpful in charting the importance of context in the development of ethics, Aristotle's view on women's virtue could hardly be taken as life affirming for black women because he does not attribute moral virtue to women. Cannon maintains that women are moral agents, with equal capacity to develop moral virtue. So, while the influence of the Aristotelian contextual approach is signaled in Cannon's use of a black feminist/womanist lens in order to give special attention to the context of oppression that influences the development and practice of womanist virtues, it is clear that adopting this dominant Western ethical lens uncritically is not an option for Cannon. In fact, it is an ethical approach that she must critically examine.[16]

Cannon's method can be seen as reflective of a virtue ethics approach in which she uncovers a set of canonical virtues, namely, "invisible dignity," "quiet grace," and "unshouted courage," that are intrinsically connected to a womanist virtue ethic. The first virtue— invisible dignity—describes an inner knowing and innate authority that stands in the face of threats of violence against the person's sense of self or integrity. Cannon refers to a self-affirmation, which was modeled by elder women from her own community, embedded within black women that encourages them to unleash their spirits and "jump at the sun."[17] The second virtue, "quiet grace," refers to the determined stance to face threats of racism and forms of injustice with a steady resolve to resist, survive, and thrive regardless. This grace, though unspoken and perhaps in some instances seemingly "quiet" in gesture, speaks a profound message of consistent perseverance for life to the observer. The third virtue, "unshouted courage," describes a deep-rooted audacious behavior that walks in spite of fear toward justice. In an entry entitled "Womanist Virtue," Cannon defines these three womanist virtues as "the moral wisdom women of African ancestry live out in their existential context which does not appeal to the fixed rules or absolute principles of the white-oriented, male-structured society."[18] Naming some of the ways in which the "absolute principles" of the aforementioned society do not fit the lives or validate the moral agency of black women, Cannon critiques dominant ethical virtues, such as frugality. Emilie M. Townes rightly celebrates and builds upon Cannon's argument, saying,

> Cannon makes an important distinction between dominant ethics and ethics from communities of the dispossessed. Dominant or traditional ethics assumes freedom and a wide range of choices for the moral agent. Dominant ethics makes a virtue of qualities that lead to economic success: self-reliance, frugality, and industry. It assumes that the moral agent is free and self-directing, and it can make suffering a desirable norm. In Cannon's view, this understanding of moral agency is not true for African Americans. Such freedom is not available.... White supremacy and male superiority force black folks to live in a different range of freedom. In situations of oppression, freedom is not a choice; nor is self-reliance. Frugality is enforced and suffering is present, but neither is chosen.[19]

Thus, womanist virtue ethics, as developed by Cannon, centers the perspectives, stories, voices, experiences, and ethical perspectives of women of African descent and other marginalized communities, naming these as powerful resources for theo-ethical inquiry. It not only lifts up the writings and experiences of women of African descent but also validates the unique contribution that womanist ethics makes to the wider discipline in that it provides important epistemologies, ethics, and moral codes that arise out of the experience of those who have been oppressed and marginalized. "The particular usefulness of this method should enable us to use the lives and literature of Black women to recognize through them the contribution to the field of ethics that Black women have made."[20] More specifically, womanist virtue ethics not only looks for ways of establishing moral agency for women and communities of color but also uses the histories, stories, and a number of "nontraditional" sources from which womanist wisdom and morals can be gleaned.

Contrary to traditional studies in dominant ethics, Cannon writes that the goal and purpose of the womanist virtue ethical project that she has undertaken is not to prescribe a "normative ethic" but rather to truly chart an ethical guide and suggest a list of virtues—uncovered from black women's literature—that actually helps black people and black women live in the present day. She judges the success of her womanist virtue method according to whether it actually provides findings that are helpful and useful for everyday use among African American women and their communities.[21] She writes,

> What I am pursuing is an investigation; (a) that will help Black women, and others who care, to understand and to appreciate the richness of their own moral struggle though the life of the common people and the oral tradition; (b) to further understandings of some of the differences between ethics of life under oppression and established moral approaches which take for granted freedom and a wide range of choices.[22]

This sense of constructing knowledge is useful among African American women from a variety of socioeconomic, geographical, and educational backgrounds and is in keeping with an emphasis in womanist religious thought to be practical.[23]

Cannon is unapologetic in her approach and in her use of a black feminist/womanist ideological lens. Citing how few sources there were in existence in the area of Christian social ethics when she began writing that took into account black women's lived realities at the time in Christian social ethics that take into account black women's lived realities and how systematic oppression impacts the unique shaping of ethical and value systems for black women and their communities, she writes in "an attempt to add to the far too few positive records concerning the Black woman as a moral agent."[24]

The publication of *Black Womanist Ethics*, as well as the use and application of Cannon's method, has radically changed the field of theological ethics. Having set a precedent by which the life, intellectual development, and spiritual strength of black women could be valorized as sources from which epistemologies can be constructed, Cannon's model not only serves womanist ethics but also shapes a path toward growing our own gardens and offers a method that can be adapted when constructing a womanist virtue ethic that illustrates and is influenced by the values and virtues found in the work of Alice Walker.

3

Doing the Work: Building a Womanist Virtue Ethic

Building on Cannon's method of gleaning virtues and values for womanist ethics from the source of black women's literature, I show in this chapter the unique relevance of Alice Walker's voice and ethical perspective for womanist religious thought and identify various moral values interwoven in her work. More specifically, I highlight the ethical implications made by Walker that signal specific values helpful in supporting a womanist virtue ethic and contribute my own list of values that emerge from the study of Walker's work that set the frame for a womanist virtue ethic. This analysis of Walker's ethics and virtues and mine is an illustration of Emilie M. Townes's concept of the womanist dancing mind in which two or more thinkers connect in a mutual exchange of ideas and critical engagement.

In the opening chapter of *Womanist Ethics and the Cultural Production of Evil*[1] and in subsequent works, Townes displays a beautiful image of the dancing mind, conceptually painted by literary writer Toni Morrison, as the fluid movement of womanist critical engagement. Townes invites readers to enter into a movement of the womanist dancing mind by quieting themselves long enough to engage in an "intimate, sustained surrender to the company of [our] own mind as it touches the mind of another."[2] In a move that requires a womanist sense of community and a commitment to practicing mutual relationality, Townes suggests that critical engagement be experienced as a dance, sometimes fraught with tension but always pointing toward wholeness, humanness, joy, and the shared experience of thinking as pleasure. The construction of a womanist virtue ethic, then, both embodies the voice and values of Alice Walker and highlights virtues that I identify from the study of her work.

To sift both the values and virtues for the womanist virtue ethic, I adopt Cannon's three-step method and survey the literature, select nonfiction essays by Walker, for "experiential themes" that emerge from the stories, experiences, and lives of black women. The experiential themes that emerge from the survey of literature serve as a source from which to highlight ethical implications made in the literature. These implications signal particular values, which are discussed in this chapter. Analysis of specific essays focuses on ethical implications made by Walker and reveal the steps she takes when uncovering and studying women's stories in order to sift values from their lives that can assist in the process of surviving and recovering from trauma, rape, abuse, and dealing with multiple oppressions. Walker's method and the values she uncovers in her nonfiction work serve as examples of the development of a womanist virtue ethic.

Having uncovered values articulated by Walker in her nonfiction, I turn to adopting the third step of Cannon's method in order to glean specific virtues lifted from ethical implications made in Walker's work. I use a distinctively womanist lens designed to highlight the intersections of race, class, gender, sexual, and Earth justice issues to reveal additional themes in Walker's work from which virtues can be identified and examined. These virtues provide a frame for a womanist virtue ethic. While not all themes uncovered in the essays showcase each of the aspects of a womanist lens simultaneously, examples in the literature certainly reveal how race, class, gender, sexual identity, and environmental relationality are connected in the moral lives of women of African descent as they make ethical decisions and practice agency in the world. The list of virtues sifted from this analysis includes generosity, graciousness, audacious courage, compassion, spiritual wisdom, justice, and good community. Together they serve as a base for the construction of a womanist virtue ethic.

The use of the adopted womanist ethical method in this work is significant not only because it shows the usefulness of and methodological precedent set in womanist ethics by Cannon but also illustrates the impact that giving attention to experience and fulfilling the womanist task of uncovering black women's stories has on womanist ethics. Applying this method also helps to acknowledge the influence of feminist ideology found in Walker's work, as well as her insistence that black women be able to name themselves as womanist and tell their own stories.[3] By using Cannon's womanist ethical method, I try to reinforce the importance of Walker's voice for womanist ethics.

This chapter begins the process by charting themes in Walker's writings that emerge from her experience and the experiences and stories of survival that come from women.

Experiential Theme: Fragmentation as an Effect of Racism

Describing the context of racial segregation that she grew up with in rural Georgia in the 1950s and the racist laws that prohibited her family from owning land, Walker often recalls moments of her childhood when she was discriminated against. In one such passage found in the essay "Choosing to Stay at Home: Ten Years after the March on Washington,"[4] Walker narrates her experience as a child watching white children enjoy ice cream cones inside an air-conditioned drugstore and feeling alienated and left out because of segregation laws that prohibited her, or anyone who looked like her, from enjoying the same. She and her people were allowed only to enter the store, buy, and leave. Through this narration, Walker recalls her deep desire as a child to be treated with the same human dignity and respect as white children; and as she looks back to reflect upon and name her own feelings, she remembers feeling like she was in "exile in her own town."[5] Walker writes about how she perceived herself then as equally deserving of the rights and privileges of childhood, yet was forced to deal with an alternative view of herself by the society that withheld equal opportunity from her because of the color of her skin.[6] The racist ethos and practice of white supremacy in the South helped to enforce laws of segregation that reigned supreme for centuries; its legacy remains a part of America's history today. In the essay, Walker records insights on the impact racist ideology had on her self-perception and worldview. Walker's description of feeling like she did not belong and was "in exile" in her own town reveals the fragmenting effect of racism on her person and a sense of separation from her own homeland. More specifically, fragmentation as a sense of separation within the self characterizes the effect of racism and appears as a consistent experiential theme throughout Walker's work.

Evidence of this theme of fragmentation within the self is also expressed in her essay "Beyond the Peacock: The Reconstruction of Flannery O'Connor."[7] In a conversation with her mother, as they sit and talk together in a desegregated restaurant in 1974, Walker explains that her constant search for wholeness as an adult is directly tied to the sense of fragmentation that she experienced as a child. Answering her mother's question about why she so often travels back to the South, after having explored different parts of the world, and what exactly she is looking for, Walker replies, "a wholeness."[8] Suggesting that everything around her is fragmented and "split up," she explains that her search for wholeness is a result of the "split" in history, literature, and people. For the reader taking special note of experiential themes and values in Walker's writing, this passage reveals Walker's attention to the theme of fragmentation and especially the fragmenting effect on the self and society. More specifically, the passage also suggests an ethical implication sewn throughout Walker's writings that one ought to find the rootcause of racial injustice, thereby uncovering a value of wholeness.

The passage also illustrates a pattern in Walker's writing style, traditionally used by black Southern and social protest writers—presence of the problem of injustice as well as a solution or plan to eradicate it.[9] In a way that reflects Walker's sense of responsibility as a black Southern writer to "give voice to centuries not only of silent bitterness and hate but also of neighborly kindness and sustaining love,"[10] Walker both names the injustice of racism and proposes a value of wholeness to counteract the fragmenting effects of racism.

An interconnection between the person and the community is clearly apparent to Walker in that her concern about the fragmentation of individual people as a result of racism and white supremacy (the false notion that white people are racially superior, which serves to privilege whites over blacks and all other races) also suggests a concern about the fragmentation within the community and in the society at large. Peter J. Paris's argument that according to an African cosmological perspective the person and community are interdependent coincides with Walker's analysis here, indicating that whatever affects the individual, negatively or positively, also directly impacts the community. Paris explains the concept saying,

> The interdependence of individuals and the community has major implications for all human activities. For instance, since individuals are parts of the community, the latter must assume responsibility of both the good and the bad actions of the former. Thus the community celebrates the good that individuals do and, whenever their bad actions offend either some divinity or ancestor, the community must repent of those actions by offering propitiatory sacrifices to counteract the ill effects of the deed. Africans never view wrongdoing as strictly an individual matter.[11]

Noting the black empowerment and racial consciousness sentiment that filled the air and framed the historical context in which Walker was writing this essay in 1975, I contend that Walker's understanding about the individual, communal, and societal fragmenting effects of white supremacy emerged out of an African moral consciousness. Naming the dangerous effects that racism can have on the common unity and shared humanity among people, Walker maintains that it is morally wrong to create and enforce laws that limit opportunities for black people, thus restricting their access to basic human and civil rights and in effect disregarding their humanity on the basis of the color of their skin. Similar to an argument made by Paulo Freire, Walker points out that societal fragmentation affects not only black people's self-identity, self-esteem, and communal well-being, but also the identity of the dominant or metaculture as well.[12] Being unable to see and honor the full humanity of others is indicative of one's inability to see and honor the full humanity of the self. Therefore, this crux of white supremacy that leads to the separation between whites, blacks, and other peoples of color provides insight into the fragmented sense of being human that lays at the foundation of any white supremacist or internalized racist perspective.

Turning her attention to the fragmenting effects that racism can leave on a person's selfhood, Walker addresses the split within the self in the essay "The Civil Rights Movement: What Good Was It?" Here, Walker refers to her own feeling of separation from herself by using the image of a disjointed human to explain her experience as a teenager. Describing how her mind and body felt separated because of the limitations racist structures put on her desires to become a writer or scientist, Walker writes, "My mind was locked apart from the outer contours and complexion of my body as if it and the body were strangers.... I wanted to be an author or a scientist—which the color of the body denied."[13] Walker's description of her disjointed inner self is based on the feelings of "exile" and fragmentation she experienced as a youth after being excluded from pleasures and places that white children were able to enjoy. The dissonance between her self-perception, the racist perceptions of her person, and the internalized sense of exile that she experienced highlights the multiple layers of fragmentation of the self that can occur as an effect of racism and white supremacy.

The split in history and literature that Walker points to is another example of the theme of fragmentation in her work. In "Beyond the Peacock," Walker demonstrates her awareness of how racist ideology renders the history and stories of black people invisible. She further points out the skill and compassion necessary for humanity when making connections between human experiences, regardless of race, as a writer. Even when stories of human experiences are told through literature, the author can render other human experiences invisible. She signals this point in her observations about acclaimed Southern writer Flannery O'Connor. Walker admirably pinpoints her direct style of writing as courageous for that time and celebrates that even as a white Southern woman writer, O'Connor is not afraid to address some of the complexities of racial dynamics in the South. Still, Walker is not convinced that O'Connor really sees black people nor renders their own stories visible to the reading public. This can be seen through Walker's comparison of O'Connor's choice of char-acters, imagery, and use of metaphor to the work of black Southern writers, including herself.

Walker begins the essay with an uncanny and interesting obser-vation that she and O'Connor "lived within minutes of each other on the same Eatonton-to-Milledgeville road"[14] in 1952 when Walker was age eight and O'Connor twenty-eight. Walker then dives into a cultural comparison of land, life, and literature that shapes white Southern women writers differently from black Southern women writers. Clearly portraying the injustice of unequal access to land, housing inequalities, and instances in which blacks were denied land ownership over generations, in comparison to the full access to land, comfort and ownership offered to southern whites, Walker states: "I think: it all comes back to houses. To how people live. There are rich people who own houses to live in and poor people who do not. And this is wrong."[15] Walker's insistence on housing equality, her critique of white privilege, and her ethical demand that attention be given to poverty and other class issues are ethical implications recorded in the essay.

As powerful a contribution as O'Connor makes to the world of literature, from Walker's perspective, the difference of growing up black and poor in the South drastically influences Walker's writing style, making it unique and widely different from O'Connor's work. In a move that accentuates her own contribution as a black woman writer and simultaneously critiques the system of white racial privi-lege, Walker's writing clearly states an ethical demand and valuing of racial equality in literature, in history, and in society at large.

Further evidence that Walker is aware of the link between racism and the split (fragmentation) in history and literature is found in her essay "Saving the Life that Is Your Own."[16] Walker recounts her story of finding Zora Neale Hurston's name for the first time as a footnote to the work that white male scholars produced about anthropological perspectives. The tone in Walker's work indicates that while these white male scholars appeared to have valued Hurston's research, they did not value her being or her status as the scholar who conducted the research.[17] Here, Walker recognizes how racist ideology impacts the way white scholars tell black history and lifts this as an example of an attempt that some white scholars made to subversively reduce the significance of scholarly contributions by black scholars such as Hurston, or to name the contribution as their own. Walker's observation about the fragmentation in history advances the idea that racism allows white scholars (like Botkin and Puckett, whom she refers to in the quotation) to shape black history according to their own perspectives instead of honoring black people's account of their own history.[18] According to Walker, one of the impacts of racist ideology is that it renders the history, stories, and experiences of black people unimportant or invisible. This "invisiblization"[19] makes it appear as if black stories, histories, and experiences are less valuable than those that serve as resources for dominant epistemologies.[20] Suggesting an experiential theme, then, Walker points to the invisibilization of black voice and history as problematic and not in keeping with racial justice. One value that can be lifted from this is the uncovering and validation of black people's and black women's voices and stories.

A final example of how Walker addresses the split in history and literature is found in her convocation speech to the Sarah Lawrence graduating class of 1972. Here, she notes how racist ideology can be sewn into college and university curriculums simply by ignoring or not teaching the history, literature, and work of marginalized peoples, including writers of African descent. Remarking upon the irony of how knowledge is constructed in university settings, with the exclusion of true history and literature, she critiques the idea of having "superior knowledge": "That is why historians are generally enemies of women, certainly of blacks, and so are, all too often, the very people we must sit under in order to learn. Ignorance, arrogance, and racism have bloomed as Superior Knowledge in all too many universities."[21]

Implying that Sarah Lawrence (at the time) may be one of the universities that needs to take a closer look at their curriculum to ensure that history is being told accurately and from the voices of those who have traditionally been silenced, she urges her alma mater to add a year-long course on black literature to its curriculum.[22] In this way, Walker makes an ethical implication that black literature, black intellectual thought, and black history be included in the core curriculum in colleges and universities. This move acknowledges both the value of education and the value of black literature, history, and thought as part of the story of humanity.

In the section above, I have applied a womanist lens to approach literary works by Walker to illustrate how experiential themes can be gleaned from Walker's writings and uncover ethical implications in the literature. Walker makes several ethical implications, including the necessity of racial equality, housing equality, and fairness in land ownership. These and other implications promote specific values embedded in Walker's work, including the value of wholeness, racial justice, validating and making black people's voices and stories visible, education in general, and education regarding black history, literature, and black intellectual thought in particular. Noting the significance of the value of wholeness for both the individual and the community in Walker's thought, the following section dives deeper into it uncovering and validating voices and stories of women of African descent as specific contributions that Walker presents to womanist religious thought.

Value: Wholeness

The analysis of the experiential theme of fragmentation in Walker's work shows how splits in self, society, literature, and history are all linked as effects of racism and white supremacy. Following the trajectory of black women and social protest writers, Walker does not simply raise certain points of analysis on issues of justice. She provides clear ethical implications and even promotes certain values that should be practiced and celebrated in individual lives and in the global community. What is important to note for the purpose of uncovering ethical implications and values from the experiential themes in Walker's writings is that within the same essays where Walker identifies the injustices and problems of society, she names solutions and values that can help eradicate injustice—in this case, reconciling fragmentation. The value of wholeness is as clear as the theme of fragmentation in these essays.

The value of wholeness first shows up in the conversation between Walker and her mother described above. Here, the sense of wholeness that Walker refers to not only connotes her attempt to heal the scars left on her own self-image and self-esteem that racism left behind;

it also connotes something much deeper—a unity of the wholeness and interconnection between all of humanity and Creation. In this regard, the term is interlaced with moral undertones and serves as an ethical implication, essentially making a claim that unity, equality, freedom, and basic rights ought to be afforded to every person and every part of creation. Most of Walker's early writings discuss the importance of human and racial equality, acknowledging the shared experiences of communities of color and giving attention to the global stretch of humanity; they also offer important dialogue points for discourse about environmental justice, including the Earth and nature as parts of the universal whole. It is for this reason that the sense of wholeness, according to Walker, extends way beyond just a connection between human, racial, or cultural circles and reaches deep into the crevices of Earth herself.

Recalling part 2 of Walker's definition that describes a womanist as one "committed to survival and wholeness of entire people, male and female," one can easily see the values of survival and wholeness that appear throughout her work. It is worthy of note that wholeness in this case is gender-inclusive, thus signaling a gender-inclusive lens in womanist religious thought. Though woman centered in her worldview and certainly influenced by feminist, black feminist, and womanist ideals, Walker refuses to conform to a female-only and anti-male approach found in some feminist perspectives.[23] It is crucial to recognize the kind of gender inclusivity that Walker refers to in describing her sense of wholeness in part 2 of her definition because it shows how this value dovetails into other values held by Walker, including the uncovering of black people's (women's and men's) history and her-story. Walker's inclusion of "male" in the womanist definition is itself an ethical implication of the gender inclusivity in her understanding of wholeness. It suggests that women *and* men ought to fight for gender, racial, economic, sexual, and environmental justice in African Diasporic communities around the globe. It is not just up to women to usher forth gender justice and equal rights and promote agency while fighting for the sacredness of the Earth. Men must be engaged in this work too. Walker's inclusion of black men's voices, lives, and experiences for womanist inquiry is significant because it serves as a response to critiques sometimes launched by black men and others who claim that womanists are only mirroring the same kind of gender discrimination that they face. For this reason, it is important to note that Walker's sense of community and wholeness includes men.

Walker honors men in many of her writings. Indicating the important influence that male mentors, authors, and activists, such as Langston Hughes and Howard Zinn, have contributed to her journey, she writes,

> We must cherish our old men. We must revere their wisdom, appreciate their insight, love the humanity of their words. They may not all have been heroes of the kind we think of today, but generally it takes but a single reading of their work to know that they were all men of sensitivity and soul.[24]

Writing about the conflicted but eventual peaceful relationship she had with her father, Walker describes her father's influence upon her: "I thank my father for his wonderful sense of humor, which effortlessly undermined the racist nonsense that passed for white supremacist wisdom while I was growing up."[25] The sacrifices that both women and men have made throughout history that paved a path for her to become a writer is not lost on Walker. The sense and meaning of wholeness in her work becomes evident in her writing tone as she honors the gifts that people have given her in order for her to achieve her dreams and goals. The value of gratitude shows up as part of Walker's sense of wholeness as well as a life-affirming connection between she as a writer and her community. For Walker, this sense of wholeness is worth passing on.[26]

Additional examples of the value of wholeness in Walker's writings are found in "From an Interview" in *In Search of Our Mothers' Gardens*, in which she talks about her meaning of wholeness and reestablishes her commitment to it. She states, "I am preoccupied with the spiritual survival, the survival *whole* of my people. But beyond that, I am committed to exploring the oppressions, the insanities, the loyalties, and the triumphs of black women."[27] Even beyond the collection of essays in *In Search of Our Mothers' Gardens*, published in 1983, wholeness appears as a major value in Walker's writings about environmental justice, female genital mutilation, the civil rights movement, the embrace and expression of women's sexualities, and celebration of gay, lesbian, bisexual, and transgendered communities. Walker's vision of wholeness reflects a sense of inclusivity, irrespective of sexual orientation, gender identity, economic standing, color, racial background, or religion. In a word, Walker attempts to include "all the *folk*" in her understanding of wholeness, pointing to the complex and diverse ways that humans can reflect the divine while simultaneously belonging to black communities, multiple communities of color, and women's circle groups around the world. Wholeness clearly appears as a primary moral goal in her writings. The moral connotation or ethical implication in Walker's work often encourages communities to create wholeness even in the midst of facing multiple oppressions. Since the agonies of interrelated oppressions have attempted to dig into the foundation of self-worth, self-esteem, agency, and the very value of the humanity of African peoples, the moral goal of living into, being committed to and fighting for individual, communal, and Earth wholeness ("wholeness of entire people"), is an essential task for Walker's womanism.

Value: Uncovering and Validating Voices and Stories of Women of African Descent

Similar to the ways in which Walker's mentor-writers, such as Langston Hughes and Zora Neale Hurston, uncovered the rich colors and experiences of black life, Walker attempts to achieve wholeness in history, story, and literature by uncovering stories and wisdoms of women of African descent in much of her nonfiction work. This task is the premise of Walker's approach to many nonfiction essays, including "In Search of Our Mothers' Gardens,"[28] which is often cited as one of her most important and award-winning contributions to the field of literature. For Walker, the voices, experiences, and stories of women of African descent (and as we see in her later work, women and people of color from a variety of cultures around the globe) must be heard and considered a part of the universal story of literature, history, and culture. Considering the impact that racism has had on how black history is told, or not told, Walker's writings give attention to the effects of fragmentation on history and literature. Walker's work presents uncovering these stories as a necessary corrective to racial injustice.

In her essays "The Black Writer and the Southern Experience" and "The Unglamorous but Worthwhile Duties of the Black Revolutionary Artist, or of the Black Writer Who Simply Works and Writes,"[29] Walker's understanding of her responsibility to uncover and record the stories of women and peoples of African descent is revealed. Here, she describes the trademarks and responsibilities of black Southern literary writers, naming herself as part of this tradition, and explains the rich heritage that has been "bequeathed" to her:

> No one could wish for a more advantageous heritage...a compassion for the earth, a trust in humanity beyond our knowledge of evil, and an abiding love of justice. We inherit a great responsibility as well, for we must give voice to centuries not only of silent bitterness and hate but also of neighborly kindness and sustaining love.[30]

The responsibility that Walker names in this passage of "giving voice" to the experience of black people suggests that a part of Walker's identity as a black writer revolves around the value of uncovering black people's stories and the stories of women of African descent. Walker asserts that she is engaged in the important task of "simplifying history and writing it down (or reciting it) for the old folks."[31] This interconnection between the task of uncovering and the black writer's responsibility to embody and pass on history suggests that uncovering black people's and especially black women's stories is not only a value expressed in her work but also a mark of self-identity and value in her life.

Yet another example of Walker's value of uncovering appears in her essay "A Talk: Convocation 1972." In the convocation speech, Walker recounts her experience teaching history to adult learners in Mississippi and their efforts to tell their own stories. Walker shares the story of Mrs. Winson Hudson, one of the students she taught, whose courage withstood the repeated bombings of her home by the Ku Klux Klan. She relates Mrs. Hudson's desire to share her story so that other people might "know what it meant to fight alone against intimidation and murder."[32] Using Mrs. Hudson's courage to come to voice and write her story as inspiration, Walker encourages the graduates of Sarah Lawrence and especially the young black women to uncover the stories of women like Mrs. Hudson and in so doing uncover their own.

Having explored the values of wholeness and uncovering and validating the voices and stories of women of African descent in Walker's work, we move to the following section to the task of surveying the literature to highlight experiential themes and identify ethical implications from which values can be gleaned.

Experiential Theme: Dehumanization

Another important experiential theme found in Walker's work is dehumanization. According to Walker, dehumanization occurs as an effect of racism, classism, and other forms of oppression. Dehumanization is any act of negating the intrinsic value and worth of a human being; however, it is often linked to forms of violence and systematic oppression. Womanist theologian, Delores S. Williams explains how the dehumanization of women of African descent has occurred throughout history in her essay "Sin, Nature and Black Women's Bodies."[33] According to her concept of the "sin of defilement," it is a sin to defile, violate, or abuse the body, mind, or spirit of any person and more specifically any woman of African descent. Critiquing forms of hegemonic patriarchy that support the logic of domination and dualisms that separate male from female and the Earth or matter from spirit, Williams keys into a connection between women and the Earth, making a parallel between how each suffers by systems of domination. Similar to the ways in which women's bodies have historically been used, abused, and manipulated (at the hands of men and women), the body of the Earth has been destroyed in the pursuit of power, domination, control, and greed. Building upon Williams's point, I contend that the sin of defilement illuminates the meaning of dehumanization in that it eats at the very core of the divine nature and creating power of Spirit within each human being. In this regard, racism, classism, sexism, heterosexism, homophobia and all internalized versions of these oppressions are social sins that result in demeaning a human person of her/his worth and value. Just as the raping of women of African descent is a sin before God, women, the Earth, and humanity, so too is any act that dehumanizes a person, particularly because it dishonors the essence of that person, the Spirit within.

According to Walker, the racist ideology built into white supremacy that considered peoples of African descent less than human and treated them like property, and the forms of internalized racism that result in women and men of African descent violently attacking each other are examples of how African peoples have historically been dehumanized in the United States.

Explaining how dehumanization can have an impact on black people living in the present day, Walker writes in her essay "Heaven Belongs to You: *Warrior Marks* As a Liberation Film" of her own observation at the age of fifty of how African peoples as a result of having suffered "centuries-long insecurity...have a hard time believing we are lovable."[34] Recalling her observation of how African peoples fear accepting critique or learning less than "good" things about themselves, she explains that a root fear of abandonment and exposure can rest at the base of black life experience. One solution is to meet this realization with compassion. Understanding the context of racist hatred that many people of African descent have endured helps toward developing values that can bring people back to themselves, fully accepting their humanity and cherishing it. Walker describes people of African descent as "having been stolen from or expelled by Africa and rejected, as human beings."[35] Walker's theme of dehumanization signals an ethical implication of humanization and a value of self-love. In this description, Walker points to the psychological and emotional scarring left upon African peoples as a result of being ripped from the shores of Africa, surviving the middle passage, and slavery. True to form as a social protest writer, Walker not only lifts dehumanization up as a problem that African peoples have had to contend with historically in the United States but also highlights some solutions of how to combat the effects of dehumanization in order to reclaim the lives and self-worth of African Americans living in the present day.

The correlative notion of white supremacy is another example in Walker's writings that shows how dehumanization can result from racism. In her essay "The Civil Rights Movement: What Good Was It?" Walker explains how the notion of white supremacy dehumanizes black people by separating them from positive images of themselves. Recalling how her mother used to watch soap operas featuring white actors who played "Beautiful White People" on television, Walker writes about her dismay after witnessing the way television images of white beauty and affluence made her mother temporarily disdain her own color and wish that she were white.[36] In the passage, Walker illustrates the dehumanizing effect of racism through the conditioned inability of black people to accept themselves as fully human and of equal worth "comparable" to whites. While it is not clear whether the soap operas had overt messages of racial superiority, Walker suggests that as a black person, one runs the risk of trying (in vain) to identify with the images of white power and wealth on television, thus falling into the "Beautiful White People trap." According to Walker's analysis, this trap results in black people's questioning their own worth and value and even succumbing to the untrue belief that whites are superior human beings whereas they are "nobodies, and thus nonhuman."[37] Walker perceives the connection between racism and dehumanization to be a problem that leads to the dehumanization not only of peoples of African descent but of *all* people.

Walker writes about the negative effects of racism even when the black race is considered racially superior. Noting some of the negative impacts of the Black Power movement such as the entrenched sexism that all too often accompanied it and the insistence that only black culture be valorized as significant, Walker makes clear in her essay "The Unglamorous but Worthwhile Duties of the Black Revolutionary Artist," that though the sentiment of black pride and black dignity are important, understanding blacks as racially superior to whites, or any race is just another form of racism. Walker recalls a teaching experience in which a Black Nationalist student insisted that he shouldn't have to read the works of William Faulkner in her classroom because Faulkner was not a black writer. In the essay, Walker implies that racial superiority itself, blinds people to the positive contributions people from various racial groups, ethnicities, and cultures make to the universal human narrative and the human connections one can make by engaging each others' minds and work.[38]

Recalling the situation, she suggests that a connected system of oppressions helps to maintain the intersections between racist ideology, white supremacy, economic imbalance, poverty, and unequal access to education. The connection between racism and education is a strong one and worthy of dismantling according to Walker's ethical implications. Building upon her discussions of the fragmentation that occurs due to parts of black history and literature being erased or left out of curriculum, she declares that the solution is not to study only black figures, literature, or authors. When it comes to education, the remedy for white racism is not black racism. The answer is not to educate students solely about black literature but rather to teach them the basics about literature and show them the validity of perspectives written by black authors, the vast diversity of perspectives, and the varying genres, and styles within the field to encourage their own stories, writing styles, and voices to join in the universal project of storytelling.

The story that Walker tells in the essay "Nobody Was Supposed to Survive: The MOVE Massacre"[39] uncovers how violence is used as a tool of dehumanization. Here, she illustrates how racism, classism, and elitism converged into a violent eruption and writes about the social outrage following the city-ordered bombing of the MOVE house that resulted in "the deaths of at least 11 people, many of them women, five of them children" in Philadelphia in 1985.[40] Tenants of the house were called "radical, black, back-to-nature revolutionaries" in newspaper articles and considered a disrespectful presence by middle-class neighbors.[41] According to the essay (which includes snippets from newspapers and gruesome details from police and coroner's logs), MOVE, short for "movement," was a group of black "radical utopians" living in a black middle-class neighborhood and were "hated" by neighbors and city officials because of their different lifestyle. In the essay, Walker explains that neighbors and officials "didn't like the 'stench' of people who refused...to use deodorant...didn't like orange peels and watermelon rinds on the ground; didn't' like all those 'naked' children running around with all that uncombed hair [dreadlocks]."[42] The MOVE people's actions were, according to other black middle-class neighbors, unsanitary, poor, and "backwards." Yet deeper analysis of the situation provided by Walker suggests that complaints about MOVE's cleanliness and conduct were far from the real reason the MOVE house was bombed. Instead, Walker suggests that racism and classism were the factors that influenced the government's decision to annihilate the MOVE people. The reason for the bombing had less to do with keeping the black middle-class neighborhood clean and more to do with the fact that the MOVE people were poor and black. Her questioning of the inability of city officials and neighbors to see black poor people as fully human reemphasizes her theme of dehumanization. The story reveals the core of racism in America—the attempt to erase the humanity of black people based on a notion of white superiority—and the core of classism—the attempt to erase the humanity of poor people based on the faulty notion that wealth measures humanity.

According to Walker, MOVE people, while not middle class like their neighbors, were "capable of intelligently perceiving and analyzing American life, politically and socially...but...this was not acceptable behavior."[43] In essence, Walker suggests that racism, instigated by city officials (and perhaps intraracism by the black middle class), and classist attitudes, maintained by black middle-class neighbors, combined to form a decision against the humanity of MOVE people. "The real reason for the government hit-squad is no secret: MOVE is an organization of radical utopians. Their political activity, their allusions to Africa, their dreadlocks, all speak rejection of the system. For this, they have been...bombed."[44]

An additional theme of violence is raised in this essay by Walker's reference to the bombings by the U.S. military in Libya and Vietnam, which left thousands and thousands of civilians dead. By referencing the dehumanizing attitudes that some Americans and the American government display around the world, Walker brings attention to the global impact the American scope of dehumanization has on the rest of the world. In her writings as a social activist, Walker raises public consciousness by drawing attention to racism and classism and their link to dehumanization by alerting readers to the dangerous effect dehumanization can have as it breeds violence across the street and across the globe.

The exploration of the theme of dehumanization in Walker's work also reveals several ethical implications. Values that flow from these implications include survival and liberation. The following section discusses how these values can be identified from the ethical implications made by Walker, thus contributing two more values in constructing a womanist virtue ethic

Values: Survival and Liberation

In keeping with the style of social protest writing and her pattern of mentioning an injustice and providing a solution/justice response to an ethical dilemma at the end of the narration, the MOVE essay professes the value of survival. The title itself, "Nobody Was Supposed to Survive," indicates that despite the violence they employed to annihilate all MOVE members in the house, there was indeed a survivor: "There was only one adult survivor of the massacre: a young black woman named Ramona Africa."[45] Walker does not imply that the survival of Ramona Africa will lead her (or anyone else) to an ultimate redemptive process of liberation.[46] However, the mere fact that she did survive suggests that regardless of the depth of dehumanization and oppression used against black people, people of color in general, and all poor people, they will and do find ways to survive and resist oppression. Relying on the powerful sense of hope that lives on through Africa's survival in the story, Walker is careful not to overemphasize the value of survival in the essay. Rather, she allows the proof of Ramona Africa's life to speak for itself.

The value of survival shows up in other essays as well in which Walker reflects upon her own experience of "making a way out of no way,"[47] growing up in a racist society but still finding wholeness as an adult. Walker's experience of racism at an early age made it necessary to be keenly aware of racial oppression and confront it accordingly; it was the only way to survive. Walker's value of survival is illustrated in her description of how black people in her community had to negotiate life around the reality of racism:

> It was understood that they [white people] were—generally—vicious and unfair, like floods, earthquakes, or other natural catastrophes. Your job, if you were black, was to live with that knowledge like people in San Francisco live with the San Andreas Fault. You had as good a time (and life) as you could, under the circumstances.[48]

This example of the mode of survival that black people had to learn suggests that white supremacist notions and ardent racism determined the ethos of the South but did not completely negate the existence of black life. Even though laws of segregation barred African Americans from having equal rights to jobs, land, and work, in essence, they *survived,* taking white racism into account but never allowing it to stop them from living and celebrating life.

Additional examples whereby the value of survival can be identified from ethical implications in Walker's writings can be found throughout her reflections on the civil rights movement. Becoming a part of the movement raised her consciousness concerning the complexities of racism in the South and changed her worldview. It was King's leadership and the movement itself that gave her and a host of other African Americans living in the South hope, self-love, self-respect, and a renewed understanding that they too were and deserved to be treated as fully human. Contrary to the mode of survival that indicated that African Americans could only "get by" and that survival was the be-all and end-all, Walker's writings about the awareness she received in the movement suggest a shift in her worldview. It was a shift from a value of survival to a value of liberation. When survival remained a crucial value in Walker's thought, it was only part of the process toward liberation. However, liberation shifts to the forefront of Walker's thought. This is particularly evident in Walker's reflections in the essay "The Civil Rights Movement: What Good Was It?" Here, Walker explains how the movement gave black people a whole sense of their human selves (self-autonomy) and validated their human worth. This empowerment encouraged many to fight for their rights to be treated as equal citizens in America and thus promoted the full humanity of black people, stopping the legal sanction of racist ideology and bringing about rights and freedom for all people of African descent.

The movement also changed Walker's personal life. She claims that it brought her to a level of awareness of her own self-worth and *beingness* and affirmed the humanity that she felt among those closest to her in her black community. By attempting to usher in a social transformation that would heal the soul of America, King and the civil rights movement led black and some white people to respond to racism by shifting the mindset of African peoples from a mode of survival to a process of being free: liberation. According to Walker, King's philosophy helped to reveal the effects of racism, dehumanization, and fragmentation on African peoples and showed all the importance of participating in the process of liberation.[49]

Observation of Walker's experience growing up in the South and becoming involved with the civil rights movement reveals the themes of fragmentation and dehumanization as effects of multiple oppressions, especially racism. By identifying ethical implications from these themes, we see how the values of survival and liberation become paramount in Walker's ethic. These values are also important for womanist ethics. So far, the literature chosen to conduct the analysis has been lifted from *In Search of Our Mothers' Gardens*. Signaling the importance of including Walker's writings from different volumes of her nonfiction work, the following section highlights themes for analysis found in *Living by the Word* and in her third collection of nonfiction essays, *Anything We Love Can Be Saved: A Writer's Activism*.

Experiential Theme: Devaluation of Women of African Descent

As an activist, Walker's ethical concern about the devaluation of women of African descent as a result of sexism and other interrelated oppressions prompts her to give attention to issues such as violence against women, the devaluation of women's bodies, and the devaluation and silencing of women's sexualities. The lens that Walker uses to confront these unjust realities in her writing can be considered a womanist analytical lens because she often lifts up the complexities that women of color deal with when facing racism, classism, sexism, heterosexism, homophobia, ageism, and other interrelated oppressions simultaneously. Examination of Walker's nonfiction essays shows that there are several influences, ideas, and analytical categories that Walker draws upon to make ethical decisions and develop ethical solutions. Four of the primary womanist categories of analysis that Walker draws upon in her analysis include race, class, gender, and sexual orientation. However, what makes Walker's work unique is a fifth category of analysis that she engages in her work for social justice regarding women's lives, namely Earth justice. If we consider first using the four primary categories familiar to womanist analysis as a frame through which to look at Walker's writings, we see a focus on Walker's thoughts on her own multiracial identity, experience of poverty, encounters with sexism, and the way she honors varied expressions of sexuality as important aspects of women's lives. Race, class, gender, and sexuality are four important categories of analysis (among others, such as colorism) that function in her approach to social issues, thus showing that Walker uses a womanist analytical lens in many of her writings that examine how justice, humanization, liberation, and wholeness for women of African descent and African peoples throughout the Diaspora can be achieved.[50]

Linking Walker's analysis with the womanist ethical method used throughout this book to highlight experiential themes is important because it helps to show Walker's attention to the devaluation of women of African descent as a theme from which specific values to oppose this reality can be gleaned for a womanist virtue ethic. According to Walker, the devaluation of women of African descent is directly connected to the prevalence of sexism—a mode of oppression that privileges maleness over femaleness, based on social constructions and gender roles that attempt to explain and relegate agency according to gender difference. In her essay "In the Closet of the Soul," Walker writes about how the mutated forms of sexism or internalized sexism result in injustice, including violence against women by women, violence against women by men, and explains how sexism and patriarchy play a role in unfairly shifting attention away from violence against black women.[51] In a passage about her own disappointment at some black male critics' review of her books *The Third Life of Grange Copeland* and *Meridian*, she explains that what most surprised her was the men's "apparent inability to empathize with black women's suffering under sexism, their refusal even to acknowledge our struggles."[52] Suggesting that the devaluation of women of African descent and their bodies occurs in part as a result of black men's refusal to become aware of their own sexism, as well as their denial that sexism exists in black communities, Walker makes an ethical call for black men to recognize their own sexist abuse as a way of healing themselves and aiding in the healing of black women and the community as a whole. Walker also records her insights and reflections about the critiques she received from black female and black male critics following the release of the film *The Color Purple*. Disappointed that many were not able to see how sexism oppresses black women in the film and in the book, Walker points out the problematic nature of how deeply entrenched sexist and patriarchal ideas operate in black communities among black women and black men, thus reinforcing an ignorance and a silencing of black women's experiences and voices. According to Walker, the devaluing of African-descended women and the choice to be ignorant and deny women's stories of having been sexually abused at the hands of persons within their own communities hinders the liberation of the community as a whole and often forces black women into silence.

"In the Closet of the Soul" was written two years (1987) after the film *The Color Purple* was released. In the reflective essay, Walker writes about the courage she had to stand in, in order to shed light on the realities of violence against women. She criticizes literary and film critics of that time for attempting to divert attention away from violence against black women and argues that in doing so they are being held responsible and are culpable for silencing the experiences, stories, and voices of countless black women. She also writes that the real reason *The Color Purple* caused so much controversy was because it exposed the reality of sexual brutality in black communities and portrayed black women as capable of being independent and of supporting themselves outside of any viable connection with men.[53] One of the most controversial aspects of the film, Walker points out, is the depiction of a loving lesbian relationship. Critics, Walker explains, interpreted this woman-to-woman loving relationship as a threat to the social system of heteropatriarchy that functions in black communities and helps support sexist hierarchies and other forms of the logic of domination. Claiming that a stand must be taken against these systems and strategies of resistance developed, Walker moves to continually unleash the voices of women as a way of releasing the truth and finding solutions that can bring an end to violence. The ethical implication in this essay is clear. Walker implies that much of the critique about her book and the movie *The Color Purple* was offered as a way of attempting to reestablish the foundation of sexism that denies the value of African and African American women's lives. Refusing to accept these established hierarchies and in resistance to them, Walker reengages her argument that black women are agents of power who can survive sexist brutalities and still love themselves, regardless.

Walker's review of *The Autobiography of David Hillard and the Story of the Black Panther Party* by David Hillard and Lewis Cole reveals that the theme of devaluation is a dominant one in the work, which is evidenced in the demeaning ways in which the bodies of women of African descent are treated. Walker compares Hillard and Cole's book to *A Taste of Power* by Elaine Brown. Noting Brown's account of how she rose to power in the Black Panther Party and the sexual intimacies and sexual violence she endured as part of that process, Walker points out that violence against women's bodies is interconnected with an imbalance of power and manipulative notions of control.[54] Women's bodies are seen as nothing more than punching bags for someone else's emotional trauma and lack of self-control, their personhood rendered invisible and their beings ripped open by abuse.

Violence against women as a form of devaluation is one of the most pronounced themes in Walker's nonfiction writings. Walker exposes the reality of black men's abuse of black women and signals that violence against women can also occur at the hands of other black women.[55] While she acknowledges that Brown, at times, had some agency in her sexual liaisons, Walker observes that Brown was used sexually. Noting the ways in which Brown did and did not have agency in the midst of the abusive paradigm, the ethical implication that Walker makes is clear: regardless of the agency that Brown had, abuse is wrong.

The image of Brown's black body being struck by a bullwhip at the hands of a member of the Black Panther Party in the essay is telling. It suggests, most vividly, that violence against black women is infused with an internalized oppression present in the soul of the abuser. The image of the abuse that Brown suffered bears a striking resemblance to torture used to "punish" African slaves during the era of American slavery. Instead of white slave owners being the bearers of bullwhips, Brown's story and Walker's inclusion of it in this essay exposes the brutal reality that the slave masters' violence is ingested, mimicked, and pressed upon the bodies and lives of black women often by the hands of their "partners" in justice, be they women or men.

The eerie similarity between a white slave owner's racist, dehumanizing, and body-breaking act of violence against an African slave woman and present-day acts of sexual, emotional, psychological, spiritual, and physical violence against the body, person, and spirit of a black woman at the hands of a black man or woman is not lost on Walker. She makes the connection clear in her essay "In the Closet of the Soul," basing her argument on the premise that just as white Southern slave owners did not see African slaves as fully human, some black men and women do not see themselves or other black women as fully human. In essence, in the eyes of some black men and women, neither women's persons nor their bodies are valued. Any act of violence against women of African descent suggests that this reality exists. Walker articulates this point by connecting themes of dehumanization to the internalized racism that descendents of black slaves have unfortunately inherited.

At the root of the denial of easily observable and heavily documented sexist brutality in the black community...is our deep, painful refusal to accept the fact that we are not only the descendants of slaves, but we are also the descendants of slave owners. And that just as we have had to struggle to rid ourselves of slavish behavior, we must as ruthlessly eradicate any desire to be mistress or "master."[56]

Walker's analysis of violence against women of African descent, the devaluation of their bodies, and the forces of dehumanization suggests a clear ethical stance regarding violence against women and raises the important values of humanizing black women and seeing their bodies as having innate and intrinsic value.

* * *

Having gained a more global perspective since the publications of *In Search of Our Mothers' Gardens* and *Living by the Word*, Walker's third collection of essays reveals an expansion of Walker's activist concerns to include justice for marginalized women across the globe. One of the social issues that she writes extensively about is female genital mutilation (FGM)—a rite of passage in which young girls endure a nonclinical procedure of having their clitoris cut away. This is a cultural tradition signifying entrance into womanhood in some African cultures and in some cases (not all) is considered to have religious significance. Walker describes the ritual as an act of violence against young African girls, cementing the devaluation of African women and strengthening the sexism evident in many African societies. Recording some of her reflections on why the tradition is allowed to continue, Walker recounts in her essay "Heaven Belongs to You: *Warrior Marks* As a Liberation Film" her witness of the procedure and interviews with girls, mothers, and practitioners who performed the rite.

In the essay, Walker focuses on the violent act of FGM and how it reinscribes the devaluation of girls' and women's bodies. The ritualistic act can leave women incapable of enjoying sexual pleasure and may lead to painful and permanent damage to women's vulvas. The procedure has also been known to contribute to life-threatening conditions that have resulted in loss of life. During Walker's years researching the rite of passage, she interviewed countless African girls and their families about the dangers, oppressive connotations, and cultural importance of the tradition; Walker also interviewed highly respected women who act as practitioners.

The very analysis of the ritual presents the significance of the theme of devaluation of the bodies of women and African girls. Furthermore, when combined with information about the cultural and economic context in which the procedure is conducted, other reasons for conducting the procedure and maintaining the patriarchal custom becomes evident. In response to her interviews with practitioners, Walker calls forth the compassion she is able to show the ritual practitioner during the interview. By recognizing "the limitations of her life, the choices thrust upon her by her society, a society deadly to women...her ignorance, deliberately enforced by the patriarchal nature of her culture,"[57] Walker makes an ethical implication that it is the injustices of poverty, the imbalance of power between men and women, and governmental structures that often lock women into systems of oppressions.

In her essay "Brothers and Sisters," Walker connects her own story to the work of ending oppression against women by examining her experience of having a black female body and living in the midst of black Southern culture in the 1940s and 1950s. The inclusion of her own story provides additional insight into the ways sexism, patriarchal hierarchies, and devaluation of girls' and women's bodies and sexualities are a global problem, and not an issue relegated to only certain parts of the African Diaspora.

> We lived on a farm in the South in the fifties, and my brothers, the four of them I knew (the fifth had left home when I was three years old), were allowed to watch animals being mated. This was not unusual; nor was it considered unusual that my older sister and I were frowned upon if we even asked, innocently, what was going on. One of my brothers explained the mating one day, using words my father had given him: "The bull is getting a little something on his stick," he said.... I believe my mother's theory about raising a large family of five boys and three girls was that the father should teach the boys and the mother teach the girls the facts, as one says, of life. So my father went around talking about bulls getting something on their sticks and she went around saying girls did not need to know about such things. They were "womanish" (a very bad way to be in those days) if they asked.[58]

Walker's experience of learning about sex and sexuality suggests that the power imbalance between men and women (the root of sexism) directly ties to the way boys and girls are taught about sexuality. In the passage above, she indicates that her father placed higher value on the expression of black male sexuality than he (or her mother) did on the expression of black female sexuality. By favoring the sexual "needs" of his sons and ignoring the sexual blooming of his daughters, Mr. Walker gave more freedom to his sons than his daughters to express their sexual selves.

Deeply rooted in the devaluation of black women's sexuality is the devaluation of black women themselves. Walker addresses this fact, pointing to her father's colorful metaphor about male sexuality. As he was teaching his sons to express and have ownership of their sexuality,[59] he implied that it was acceptable to objectify women's bodies as "somethings" to "get on their sticks." The fact that Mr. Walker's colorful metaphor did not consider the impact his sons' actions might have on women's personhood suggests that he did not consider women as valuable as men.

The sexism that permeated Mr. Walker's view planted seeds of sexism in his sons and impregnated his daughters with the fear of their own sexuality. According to Walker's writing, Mr. Walker thought that "all young women [were] perverse...[and] was always warning her [sister] not to come home if she found herself pregnant."[60] The negative perception that Mr. Walker held about young women, along with his use of fear to scare his daughter Ruth into firmly controlling (if not disregarding) her sexuality, suggests that he did not value black women's sexuality. This combined with the prevalence of sexism, maintained in the wider black Southern culture, contributed to Alice Walker's worldview concerning the worth and value of black women. It was not until she reached college and was introduced to feminist thought that she was able to understand her father's sexism.[61]

In "Brothers and Sisters," the theme of devaluation of black women and their bodies arises out of analysis of Walker's experience of sexism. While Walker's father was teaching his sons about their right and "need" to have sex with women (through the objectification of women's bodies), neither he nor Walker's mother was teaching their daughters anything about their own sexualities. Mrs. Walker's response to inquiries about women's sexuality—"She went around saying girls did not need to know about such things"—helped maintain a system of oppression by silencing stories about black women's sexuality and women's experiences in general. Walker further implies that her mother's silence about sexuality sealed the devaluation of that part of a woman's self and life story. Ultimately, this lack of knowledge about sexuality presented a power imbalance between the Walker boys and the Walker girls that sent a clear message of the devaluation of black women's sexuality.

As is shown at the end of the essay, it was not until Walker's embrace of feminist thought that she also began to uncover the impact silencing women's stories has on women. Her ethical implication is that feminist approaches allowed her and many others to embrace the liberating power of women's stories. As has already been discussed, this act of embracing women's stories is a significant value in Walker's writings that is itself an act of resistance to the oppression of sexism.

Value: Honoring Women's Sexualities and the Act of Self-Naming

Walker's analysis of the silencing of the stories and voices of women of African descent concerning sexuality and women's stories in general is an act to promote and value the uncovering of these stories. However, beyond this, the analysis suggests that careful attention be given to the valuing, education, and expression of African, African American, and all women's sexualities. Walker used the term "womanist" first in 1979;[62] and later articulated the definition in 1983. It is important to note the significance of both these descriptions of "womanist" when examining womanist understandings of sexuality and the acceptance of and freedom to express black women's sexuality that exist therein. Unlike the restricting sense of sexuality taught by her parents and contrary to societal conditioning that devalues black women's sexualities that she experienced growing up, Walker's definition of "womanist" advances the value of the healthy expression of black women's sexual identities. Her inclusion of homosexual, heterosexual, and bisexual love, as modes through which womanists can express their sexuality, suggests that Walker honors varied forms of sexuality as avenues through which women of African descent can be wholly themselves. The second part of the definition reads, "Womanist...A woman who loves other women, sexually and/or nonsexually....Sometimes loves individual men, sexually, and/or nonsexually." Through the acceptance of many forms of black women's (and all women's) sexuality, Walker states that her perspective on sexuality honors multiple expressions.

Furthermore, in her essay "All the Bearded Irises of Life: Confessions of a Homospiritual,"[63] Walker acknowledges her own attraction to women as well as men and explains her understanding of how same-gender relationships can sometimes liberate women from the bonds of sexism in heterosexual relationships and patriarchy in society. "It was no mystery...observing heterosexual relationships every day in which women are oppressed or routinely denied the full expression of who they are simply because of their gender—why women who wished to do so were right to choose other women as lovers."[64] Noting too that woman-to-woman loving and lesbian relationships can be infused with sexism, patriarchal notions, violence, and crippling forms of abuse, Walker's writing leaves room for thinking about how to confront heterosexism and homophobia in their societal, external, and internalized forms. The ethical implications within Walker's writings suggest that honoring black women's sexuality can allow women to express the wholeness of their humanity and in so doing resist oppression; but her point also reminds one of the constant vigilance necessary to be sure that deeply entrenched invisible, internalized forms of oppression do not strangle the wisdom of wholeness and commitment to honor one another's humanity regardless of the relationship.

The value of women honoring sexuality evident in Walker's writings also plays a role in the process of self-naming in the lives of women of African descent. This can be seen in the essay "Audre's Voice" in *Anything We Love Can Be Saved*.[65] Here, Walker recalls a conversation with black feminist Audre Lorde, who inquires as to whether "womanist" was designed to cause a rift within black feminism. Walkers explains the likenesses and distinctions between womanist and black feminist, pointing to two essential themes, the honoring of black women's sexuality and the necessity for black women to name themselves. Similar to the feminism that Walker learned about in college, her definition of "womanist" connotes independence from both patriarchal constructions and racist definitions and categories established by some white women. This latter value that highlights the importance for black women to name themselves is essential to incorporate in a study of womanist ethics.[66]

While the debate continues among womanists about whether to accept the second part of Walker's womanist definition dealing with sexuality, the value of honoring the sexualities of women of African descent has significantly shaped womanist religious thought.[67] The full acceptance of black women's sexualities in her definition and in her other writings suggests that the value be considered a critical element in Walker's own ethics and helpful for a womanist virtue ethic that takes Walker's own work and thought seriously.

Examination of Walker's book review "Gifts of Power: The Writings of Rebecca Jackson" is also crucial for an understanding of the origins of and emphasis on self-naming interlaced in Walker's meaning and definition of womanist. Pointing to black women's need to name themselves and highlighting the depth and complexity of black women's relationships with one another, Walker's essay suggests that the value of black women's naming of themselves strengthens their own sense of personal power, freedom, worth, and value.[68] In the review of *Gifts of Power*, edited by Jean McMahon Humez, Walker summarizes the contents of the book about a nineteenth-century black woman preacher named Rebecca Jackson. Jackson began her independent ministry late in life, outside of the official sanction of the African Methodist Episcopal church after confronting and resisting forms of sexism and patriarchy that would not allow her to lead in the church. Making a bold step to leave behind systems of patriarchy that did not support her ministry, Jackson became a Shaker eldress. *Gifts of Power* includes Jackson's writings detailing her journeys and her close relationship with another black Shaker eldress named Rebecca Perot. Walker critiques Humez for presuming and naming the relationship between Jackson and Perot as a lesbian relationship. Though Walker affirms lesbian sexual orientation, she notes that Humez's quick attempt to name and identify the relationship between these black women as solely sexual is problematic. Walker points out that Jackson speaks clearly throughout her writings about her commitment and desire to practice celibacy, thus revealing a blind spot on the part of Humez, who may have attempted to apply a stereotypical category to the relationship between the women without honoring the actual voices of the women and how they named and identified themselves. The ethical implication that Walker makes in this point, then, reveals the danger of allowing nonblack scholars to name black women according to their own categories, without acknowledging the complexity of relationships between black women, sexual and otherwise. Expressing the various "womanist" ways black women can relate to each other, Walker critiques Humez:

> There is only one point at which I stopped.... It is when she discusses the relationship between Rebecca Jackson and Rebecca Perot (known among the Shakers as "the two Rebeccas").... One wonders why, since Jackson mentions more than once her "deadness" to sexuality or "lust," Humez implies she was a lesbian?...The women did not accept this label when it was made, and I think we should at least wonder whether they would accept it now, particularly since the name they *did* accept, *and embrace*, which caused them so much suffering and abuse, was *celibate*.[69]

The reason Walker critiques Humez is because she places a label on Jackson that may not fit. Explaining that black women's relationships with each other push way beyond traditional categories of sexuality used by Humez, Walker asserts that the relationship between Rebecca Jackson and Rebecca Perot may simply and most profoundly be an example of a *womanist* relationship. Emerging from this critique is

Walker's ethical implication that nonblack scholars often try to lodge black women into particular categories without listening to black women's description and experiences of being themselves. The value that emerges from this ethical implication is self-naming, and it is rooted in Walker's argument that black women must name themselves, separate and apart from what others say about them, or how others may try to force them to accept a name or identity that is not true and does not fit.

*   *   *

Analysis of selections from Alice Walker's nonfiction writings reveals three experiential themes, namely, fragmentation, dehumanization, and the devaluation of women. In keeping with a womanist ethical method whereby black women's literature is used as a source from which to lift experiential themes, highlight ethical implications, and glean values that help build a womanist virtue ethic, this chapter presents the values of wholeness, uncovering and validating voices and stories of women of African descent, survival and liberation, honoring women's sexualities, and the act of self-naming that serve as parts of a womanist virtue ethic. In addition, these values and the analysis of them can serve as ethical guideposts for women looking to craft their own ethical ways of being and thinking in the world.

In keeping with the womanist ethical method, the next chapter adds to the list of values uncovered in this chapter by surveying additional nonfiction essays by Walker. The analysis not only contributes six additional values to the list of canonical values found here but also reveals Walker's own ethical perspective and examines the method she herself uses to identify values from her mother's story as illustrated in two essays, "Saving the Life That Is Your Own: The Importance of Models in the Artist's Life" and "The Black Writer and the Southern Experience."

4

Stay on the Path, Walk the Journey:
Values to Hold On

Alice Walker does not claim to be a trained theological ethicist familiar with the details of womanist ethical methodologies used to help chart virtues and values helpful in living everyday life. However, it is precisely her attention to method that makes her work an excellent resource for womanist ethics. Remarkably similar to and perhaps being a source of inspiration to the womanist methodological approach of Katie G. Cannon, which was designed to lift virtues and values from themes in the lives and writings of women of African descent, Walker exhibits an approach in her writing that privileges the voices and stories of African American women. To honor Walker's ethical voice and perspective as a resource for womanist religious thought, this chapter discusses in detail her methods.

As a literary writer, Walker makes use of several literary methods and styles that allow her to incorporate elements of African American folklore, life, and culture in her writing.[1] It is Walker's attention to these elements—the language, rites, and values of African American culture—that has made her a prominent figure in the literary world and makes her work a primary resource for the study of womanist ethics. Walker's literary styles are a major contribution to womanist religious scholarship because they rely less on limited theo-ethical Christian categories and more on organic cultural themes that arise out of the richness of African American life and express the religious diversity experienced and practiced in African American communities.

Although Alice Walker is most widely known in womanist religious circles for her womanist definition and her fiction work (especially

The Color Purple), her prolific nonfiction essays hold deep resources for womanist religious thought in that they uncover Walker's ethical voice and perspective, thus providing an ethical figure whose life of activism and activist writings provide a resource for conducting a moral biography. In addition, attention to Walker's life and ethical perspective exemplifies the interdisciplinary alignment between theo-ethical inquiry and black women's literature that Cannon describes so aptly in her work *Black Womanist Ethics*. Analysis of Walker's nonfiction collections reveals ideas that influence her ethical decision-making process, chart the steps she uses in her own activist work to help solve societal ethical dilemmas, and evaluate the criteria she uses to judge just or unjust action. Furthermore, a deeper analysis of Walker's nonfiction work helps readers discover the uncovering of an ethical imperative for Earth justice in womanist religious thought.

Walker's sense of values and her ethical perspective on several issues can be found in most of her work, and especially in select essays in *In Search of Our Mothers' Gardens: Womanist Prose* (1983), *Living by the Word* (1988), and *Anything We Love Can Be Saved: A Writer's Activism* (1997). Analysis of select essays from each of these nonfiction collections helps reveal the steps Walker uses when addressing personal and societal ethical dilemmas revolving around issues of justice, human, animal, and natural rights. Studying these steps sheds light on Walker's ethical stance and perspective and provides an opening to understand her rich ethical thought life as a model for womanist ethics.

Alice Walker's Six-Step Approach to Ethical Issues

Six steps that Walker takes to approach ethical issues can be gleaned from examination of these essays: "Brothers and Sisters," "Nuclear Madness," and "Only Justice Can Stop a Curse." As we have already seen in previous analysis, Walker talks about the ethical dilemma of sexism and its impact on African American family systems in the first essay. In the second work, her ethical stance of nonviolence is made clear as she writes to convince readers and government officials of the unwise and unjust use of nuclear weapons. The third essay mentioned above discusses her ethical imperative for Earth justice and insists that readers take seriously the unjust treatment of the Earth. The six steps that can be observed from Walker's approach to these ethical issues are as follows: (1) to uncover the experiences and stories of black women and black people; (2) to validate these experiences and stories; (3) to ascertain values and moral lessons from critical reflection on these experiences and stories; (4) to connect values collected to wisdom that can be lived out in the present day; (5) to take action upon the wisdom and values found in the work and (6) to be empowered by these actions taken in order to create sustainable movements toward justice.

Step One: Uncover Experience and Stories

In the essay "Choosing to Stay at Home: Ten Years after the March on Washington," Walker addresses the ethical dilemma of racism and its disjointing, dehumanizing effect on people. Walker's step of uncovering experiences of black women is illustrated through the telling of her own story and experience encountering racism while living as a black girl in Georgia during the Jim Crow era. Describing her feelings of being left out and "exiled" from society as a child, Walker critiques legalized segregation and explains how racism mutated her sense of self and left her feeling fragmented from the wider society.[2] This theme of fragmentation as an effect of racism has already been discussed in chapter 3, along with several values, including wholeness, gleaned from the ethical implication that Walker makes for racial equality. What is important to note here is how the process of uncovering the experiences and stories of black women and black people directly opens the door to revealing values, virtues, and moral lessons that help Walker make conclusions about whether racism is ethical or not.

Step Two: Validate Experience

This step is made explicit through Walker's commitment to digging up and re-presenting the life and writings of Zora Neale Hurston as a noteworthy figure in the black women's literary movement. Walker's validation of Hurston's work is presented in "Looking for Zora."[3] It can also be seen in her memorable dedication to *I Love Myself When I Am Laughing...and Then Again When I Am Looking Mean and Impressive*,[4] an edited volume of Hurston's work. Here, Walker writes one of the most famous phrases about uncovering the work of black women literary artists, which both validates and honors Hurston's life experience as it is connected to the African American heritage: "We are a people. A people do not throw their geniuses away. And if they are thrown away, it is our duty as artists and as witnesses for the future to collect them again for the sake of our children, and, if necessary, bone by bone."[5] By authenticating Hurston's work, literary voice, and identity as a cultural critic and public scholar, Walker not only recaptures Hurston's anthropological method and literary writings, but also recasts them as valid sources of academic and literary study. This act gives authority to Hurston's life experience as a black woman and validates her work as a scholar.

Step Three: Ascertain Values from Critical Reflection of Experience

According to Walker, the experiences and stories of survival that emerge from critical reflection on black women's and black people's experiences are a rich repertoire of virtues and values that will help African American women navigate the structural systems of racism, classism, sexism, and heterosexism. Walker's application of this step is made evident in the essays "The Black Writer and the Southern Experience" and "Saving the Life that Is Your Own: The Importance of Models in the Artist's Life."[6] Here, Walker narrates the story of her mother's survival during a winter in the 1930s. The story takes place in a winter season during the Great Depression when rations of food were being provided by the government for families in need. After walking to town from their rural home, several children in tow, Mrs. Walker first visited the post office, where she received a package from a family relative in the North. In the package was a dress, and though worn, it was a special gift that Mrs. Walker decided to wear on that very day. Next, Mrs. Walker proceeded to the government line. When she got to the front of the line, a white woman in charge made a sly comment about her dress and then in a racist and somewhat jealous manner turned Mrs. Walker away, claiming that a woman dressed so fine did not deserve aid from the government. The white woman was required by law to give Mrs. Walker the food; but, according to Walker's tone of writing, it was the white woman's racist attitude, combined with a jealous rage and envy of the economic privilege that the woman assumed Mrs. Walker had, that resulted in Mrs. Walker's being forced to walk away humiliated, without immediate recourse, and empty handed toward her children.

After being denied governmental assistance and food, Mrs. Minnie Lou Walker was forced to "make a way out of no way" to care for herself and feed her family. Wisdom, communal sharing, and foresight, which propelled her to stock up on provisions ahead of time, were the values that helped her and her family survive the winter.

Good community, mutuality in relationship (communal interdependence), communal sufficiency, being resourceful in spite of oppression, self-reliance, and letting go for the sake of survival are the values gleaned from Walker's brief but powerful analysis of her mother's story (which are explained in detail below). She writes,

> In this small story is revealed the condition and strength of a people. Outcasts to be used and humiliated by the larger society, the Southern black sharecropper and poor farmer clung to his own kind and to a religion that had been given to pacify him as a slave but which he soon transformed into an antidote against bitterness. Depending on one another, because they had nothing and no one else, the sharecroppers often managed to come through "all right."[7]

Examination of the survival stories of African American women, in this case, Alice's mother Mrs. Minnie Lou Walker, is an important approach in womanist ethics. Though Walker does not use Cannon's specific steps of retrieving virtues and values from black women's voices, experience, and stories, her own commitment to uncover values helpful for women of African descent living in the present day sheds light on Walker's method and her ethical values.

Values

Good Community Community here can be described as a group of persons and things that share a common identity, place, or environment. The descriptor "good" indicates that community is infused with fair systems of accountability that promote the well-being of all included in the community and shared responsibility among those living and depending upon each other as they live from day to day in a common environment. Good community can be gleaned as a value in Walker's writing by her description of the common economic status of the sharecroppers' families, including her own. Considered "outcasts" by the larger society, Walker implies, that it was precisely the shared identity of being cast out of society that created a strong bond between members in the community. In an attempt to resist the negative portrayal of black people as not belonging, Walker reclaims the characteristic of her people as independent and self-sustaining. Highlighting their "strength" to endure the conditions of poverty and yet maintain a sense of shared humanity, Walker celebrates the bonds that unify her good community. One of the primary strengths that

Walker names in this passage that helps to keep members of the community together, in good stead and accountable to each other, is love. Whether providing each other with the inspiration to vote, resist racial injustice, or work together to build a schoolhouse (a project that Walker's father is known to have led),[8] the value of good community gleaned from Walker's work undergirds a humanizing, loving, and respectful nature of people in her community.

Analysis of Walker's experience growing up in this community indicates that although oppressions did exist on the outside, one way black people affirmed their own humanity and sense of self was by treating one another well on the inside of the community and maintaining a sense of belonging and togetherness. At the same time the value of community connotes togetherness, it also acted as a mode of resistance that black sharecropping communities used to respond to the social injustices of poverty and racism.

By good community, Walker also refers to belonging in her essay "The Unglamorous but Worthwhile Duties of the Black Revolutionary Artist." In this essay, Walker points to the value of good community as it is expressed in the works of black Southern writers and Southern culture. Addressing the difference between the styles of white Southern writers and black Southern writers, she states that black writers are bequeathed "a compassion for the earth, a trust in humanity beyond our knowledge of evil, and an abiding love of justice."[9] Walker's use of the words "humanity," "love," and "justice," as well as the two phrases "compassion for the earth" and "a trust in humanity," implies that a shared respect for humanity practiced by black people in the community and a communal relationship between black Southerners and the Earth are aspects of living into and upholding the values of good community. This latter point is especially important because it uncovers a principle of caring for the Earth embedded within the heritage of African peoples and written about by black Southern writers. Walker's inclusion of the Earth in her ethical system shows that the value of good community is not limited to human beings' interaction with one another. In her essay "Everything Is a Human Being," she describes an ethical assertion that all of Creation should be treated as fully human and so honored so that the Earth might be saved from greed. Naming nuclear war as a looming threat that may destroy the Earth, Walker claims that despite the multiple oppressions she faces as a black woman, even her status does not measure to the debased status that the Earth endures.[10]

Calling the Earth itself the "nigger of the world," making the point that the Earth suffers an even worse fate than those who struggle against racial hatred and injustice, Walker draws a connection between human experiences of race, class, and gender oppressions and the abusive oppressions that the Earth faces. She also points out an important link and mode of solidarity between people of color and the Earth.[11] In the essay, Walker calls for an alternative sense of freedom that includes the struggle of the Earth to survive and charges her readers to recognize the Earth as a part of the community, a being to which all things are connected. This freedom, based on interdependence and the interconnectedness between the Earth, nature, and all living things, including humans, liberates all beings and the Earth, according to Walker. The value of good community is reinforced, then, as Walker explains her belief in the web of all existence and encourages readers to act in the spirit, sharing a role of community that includes the Earth and humanity.[12] In this essay, to save human lives, the Earth, and uphold the value of good community, Walker makes an ethical implication that if indeed humans have been chosen, and most times select themselves as the "representatives" for the rest of the universe, social action for Earth justice is imperative.[13]

Mutuality in Relationship: Communal Interdependence Building on the value of good community, Walker's brief reflections about the genius of her mother's ability to quickly improvise in order to provide for her family, in spite of the white woman's racist behavior, signals another important value, the value of mutuality in relationship. Casting aside any feelings of pride or embarrassment, Walker's mother appears in the story to almost immediately shift gears into creating a solution to the problem of having no flour for the winter. Referring to the built-in trust and concern that community members had for one another, Walker describes the value of mutuality in relationship between her mother and community members as essential for her mother's ability to see her family through hard times. In the quote cited above, "Depending on one another, because they had nothing and no one else, the sharecroppers often managed to come through 'all right,'"[14] the "all right" does not indicate that an abundance of resources or plenty was magically made available but rather that community members took seriously the Christian commandment of "loving thy neighbor" and lived accordingly.[15]

Depending upon and caring for one another was not done just to adhere to a holy commandment. Rather, as Walker implies, these were followed for the sake of keeping members of the community alive and safe from acts of racial violence. According to Walker, there existed a sense of safety and trust within the sharecropping community of her youth (and in black Southern culture as a whole) that was normally not felt among white people outside their community. Recalling the general mistrust that most members in her all-black community had about white people, she writes, "There was not one white person in the county that any black person felt comfortable with. And though there was a rumor that a good white woman, or man, had been observed sometime, somewhere, no one seemed to know this for a fact."[16] Through the racism expressed by the white woman and the phrase "they had nothing and no one else," we can see that the value of mutual relationship is part of Walker's reflection on and analysis of her mother's story.

Another example of this value in Walker's writings is found in "The Unglamorous but Worthwhile Duties of the Black Revolutionary Artist." Here, she writes about a communal interdependence experienced between "black revolutionary writers" and everyday black folks. Arguing that the role of a revolutionary black writer involves more than bearing a popular title given to some who wrote novels, histories, and other texts that celebrated black life during the 1960s, Walker indicates that real revolutionary writers should be concerned about the wholeness and well-being of community. Describing the communal interdependence shared between writers and community members, Walker's writing reflects an ethical imperative for black writers to "stay close enough to them [community] to be there whenever they need you."[17] Walker's instruction for writers to "stay close" indicates that similar to the community of black sharecroppers that she grew up with, revolutionary writers depended upon each other, as well as on the black community, to help tell "real" black history and share real lived stories in ways that both young and old folks in the community could relate to, confirm, and understand.

Communal Sufficiency Walker's reference to black Southern sharecroppers as people of strength because they were able to build mutual relationships and depend upon one another suggests a value of communal sufficiency in the story. The multiple forms of oppression, including racism, classism, and sexism, that Mrs. Walker faced and that the community dealt with on a daily basis meant that the entire community had to have resources that would enable them to rely upon themselves. In a day and time when even medical help from white Southerners was not dependable,[18] Walker's writings suggest, the value of communal sufficiency was of the upmost importance. In the essay "Beauty: When the Other Dancer Is the Self," she recounts a story about the community midwife. Regardless of whether she could be paid for her services, "there was never any question that the midwife would come when she was needed, whatever the eventual payment for her services."[19] Mrs. Walker recalls that all eight of her children were born with the help of a black midwife, which is evidence for the midwife's ability to successfully bring life into the world, and thus aid the growth of the community and maintain its desire to rely upon itself and be sufficient. The pride that Mrs. Walker takes in sharing this story and Alice Walker's decision to include it in the essay show the significance of community sufficiency as an important value in her work.

The account of Walker's birth signals another example of the value of communal sufficiency and its impact on Walker's sense of activism as an adult. In the essay "The Only Reason You Want to Go to Heaven Is Because You Have Been Driven out of Your Mind (off Your Land and out of Your Lover's Arms) Clear Seeing Inherited Religion and Reclaiming the Pagan Self," Walker recalls the story of her baptism at the age of seven. Walker's memory of feeling "mud, leaves, rot, and bullfrog spoors" between her toes and the uplifting sense of her whole community waiting above the water to see her "saved head reappear" illustrates the value of communal sufficiency in that the community is shown to be more than enough for the young Walker to believe in.[20] While members of the black sharecropping community that she knew intimately as a child still had to face racism, economic injustice, and multiple forms of oppression, the communal support and presence that they provided one another was sufficient to bring about wholeness to the world she knew and the world she would come to know. She writes, "This experience of communal love and humble hope for my well-being was my reality of life on this planet."[21] Calling attention to the tangible sense of love and community that surrounded her as she arose from the murky, muddy water, Walker points out that it was not her memory of the Christian doctrine of baptism that was so important to her. Rather, it was the experience of the loving presence of community and nature that left an indelible imprint on her person and gave her a comforting presence that has remained with her.

Being Resourceful in Spite of Oppression There are at least three places in which the value of being resourceful in spite of oppression appears in the passage in which Walker records her reflections on her mothers' story. Noting the generosity of her Aunt Mandy, who shared a portion of her surplus flour with Mrs. Walker as a way of helping her get by in spite of the racism she faced, Walker suggests that the generosity of others was a welcomed and shared gift offered within community. In fact, the practice of sharing for the sake of community was so common that it inspired a common-sense approach for people to have things ready, in case of an emergency. This approach, according to Walker, served her family well, helping them to survive through the winter.[22] Being resourceful in spite of oppression can also be seen as a value in the story where the package of clothes that Mrs. Walker's sister sent her from up North is mentioned. Although it is not clear from the story whether the sister living in the North was any more financially secure than her Southern sister, the status of the clothes, "in good condition, though well-worn," makes it probable that these clothes were a gift that both encouraged Mrs. Walker and enabled her to survive. The element of resourcefulness, in spite of economic oppression (poverty, in this case), illustrated here suggests that resourcefulness can be practiced by sharing what one has with family and community.

A third example of being resourceful in spite of oppression is illustrated in Mrs. Walker's ability to return home and make a way out of no way in spite of being humiliated and dishonored. Walker's mother did not return home and allow her despair or anger at the situation to stop her from finding a way to feed her family. Instead, she relied upon herself and the "womanist wisdom" that prompted her to have a "ready stand of corn" on hand in case of an emergency situation. This sense of being prepared coincides with two other values in a womanist virtue ethic—survival and good community. Being resourceful in spite of oppression allows one to survive and achieve individual and communal wholeness. In being resourceful, one puts a value into practice that creates betters existence for the self and the community.[23]

Being Self-Reliant The value of self-reliance is one of the most pronounced virtues in Mrs. Walker's story and in Walker's analysis of it. The first example of self-reliance appears in Mrs. Walker's ability to boldly confront the white woman in order to clarify her self-perception as fully human. In the dialogue, in which the white woman tries to assert authority over Mrs. Walker, perhaps simply based on the white woman's understanding that she is racially superior to Mrs. Walker, the latter claims her right to be there just as much as anyone else, replying, "I ain't *begging*." Mrs. Walker continues, "The government is giving away flour to those that need it, and I need it. I wouldn't be here if I didn't."[24] The boldness and pride in the tone that Mrs. Walker uses in the story suggest that she is clear about her identity, sure of her right to receive the flour, and deserving of respect as much as anyone else. Mrs. Walker's ability to stand firm in these convictions, even as she is confronted with hate and envy in the face of the white woman, shows a self-reliant character and clear sense of self-respect.

A second occasion in the story that reveals the value of self-reliance is Mrs. Walker's ability to immediately convert the situation of having nothing to having something for her family to eat. Mrs. Walker's ability to make a way out of no way, by relying on her own resourcefulness in the form of a ready stand of corn and the application of her womanist wisdom to trade what she had (corn) to get what she needed (flour from Aunt Mandy Aikens), illustrates Mrs. Walker's self-reliance. According to Walker, it is the passion for life that her mother and aunt embodied that helped them manage the situation. "For their lives were not about that pitiful example of Southern womanhood, but about themselves."[25] Noting how Aunt Mandy Aikens and her mother lived lives much fuller, more demanding, and more rewarding than the typical literary trope of "southern womanhood," Walker explains that even the retelling of the story is an example of self-reliance. Similar to the way in which Walker's definition of "womanist" concludes with a tone of celebration of the self—"loves herself, regardless"—this reflection ends with the reinforcing of the value of the self and being self-reliant.

Letting Go for the Sake of Survival Letting go for the sake of survival is the sixth value that analysis of Walker's mother's story uncovers. It is clearly evident that Walker's observation of her mother's ability to move on with her life despite dealing with hardship and oppression leaves an imprint on Walker:

> My mother always told this story with a most curious expression on her face. She automatically raised her head higher than ever—it was always high—and there was a look of righteousness, a kind of holy *heat* coming from her eyes. She said she had lived to see this same white woman grow old and senile and so badly crippled she had to get about on *two* sticks.[26]

The dignity that Walker's mother carries throughout the story is implied in Walker's reference to Mrs. Walker's ability to hold her "head high" throughout and beyond the racial incident. This important virtue of dignity has a theological significance linked to a moral understanding of justice. Having endured numerous acts of racism, Mrs. Walker did not allow other people's foolish actions or racist attitudes to impede her progress, diminish her own strength, or sway her direction and drive for life. In fact, a comment by Mrs. Walker included in the essay "The Black Writer and the Southern Experience" indicates that it is precisely Mrs. Walker's insistence on dignity and self-respect that contributes to her theological reflection about the incident years later. Recalling the proud look on her mother's face each time she told the story, Walker writes, "I knew she was thinking, though she never said it: Here I am today, my eight children healthy and grown and three of them in college and me with hardly a sick day for years. Ain't Jesus wonderful?"[27] Drawing a link between divine justice and the virtue of dignity, an ethical implication that Walker's writings suggest here is that regardless of the injustice justice shall win out in the end. Despite the abuses, oppressions, and mistreatment that a black woman may face in her lifetime, Mrs. Walker's story suggests, no unjust act will go unpunished. Though the virtues of compassion and forgiveness can be gleaned from the story, most importantly, Walker seems to suggest her mother's conviction that God's justice shall in the end come to pass. This knowing promotes pride and human dignity and reinforces the desire to live as best one can according to God's commandment to love and treat one another with equality and respect. The commitment to living with dignity, regardless of others' actions, the understanding of justice, and the prescription to honor one another's full humanity are all key ethical implications made in this passage.

In the essay, Walker also alludes to the "religion" of the sharecropper, Christianity, remarking upon how the Christian tenet to forgive reinforced the practice and value of letting go for the sake of wholeness in the self and in the community. However, at the same time, Walker explains that the unique sense, use, and meaning of Christian forgiveness as understood in the black community was different from the Christian tenet of forgiveness taught in white forms of Christianity in the South. Walker's writings are typically quite critical of Christianity because of the tradition's dehumanizing aspects, sexist attributes, and stories that relegate women to a less-than-human social status. Noting how black people were able to transform the nonliberating aspects of white Southern Christianity, such as disempowering interpretations of "slaves obey your masters," into a religion that supported black liberation, wholeness, and community, Walker explains how black people of the South practiced a type of Christianity that reinforced the virtues necessary for them to survive in a racist and oppressive culture. She writes, "The Southern black sharecropper and poor farmer clung to his own kind and to a religion that had been given to pacify him as a slave but which he soon transformed into an antidote against bitterness."[28] Here Walker reinforces the transformative power the sharecroppers embodied to reshape and outright change the Christianity that had often been passed on to them by slave masters and mistresses.

Letting go for the sake of survival served as an essential value practiced among black sharecroppers in her community, and for that reason Walker further explains that time and energy were not wasted on holding grudges or plotting vendettas against white people. Instead, she writes, the behavior of white racism was simply accepted as an evil in the world, something not of God, but nevertheless to be dealt with. She writes, "In those days few blacks spent much time discussing hatred of white people. It was understood that they were—generally—vicious and unfair, like floods, earthquakes, or other natural catastrophes."[29] In passages such as this, Walker suggests that she believes that black people and communities held a tremendous amount of agency in constructing their own religious beliefs and values.

Each of the six values explicated above has special significance in the life and writings of Alice Walker. As resources for womanist ethics, these values can serve as a frame from which an ethical or moral standard can be developed to help guide the lives, choices, and actions of African and African American women. These values can also help determine right and wrong behavior and guide answers to the question, what is moral or good action? Since the values of a people are often reflected in the virtues selected as key characteristics encouraged among the community and habitually practiced in individual lives often to promote wholeness, accountability, and responsibility in good community, it is appropriate to list these values along with those named in chapter 3 as values helpful in constructing a womanist virtue ethic.

Similar to the way in which Cannon argues for the use of black women's literature as a source from which ethical values and virtues can be gleaned for the practice of everyday ethical living among

African Americans, the analysis above reveals a collection of values that Walker gleans from her mother's stories that are helpful in uncovering ethical paths of living in the here and now. Thus, by returning to the source of Walker's writings, her thought, and method of gleaning values from black women's stories, we find fresh ways to think about the ethical and spiritual lives of African and African American women.

Step Four: Connect Values to Wisdom

Having identified values that emerge from Walker's writings, the fourth step that I find in Walker's approach to ethical issues links these values to moral wisdom celebrated in womanist religious thought. Moral wisdom can be defined as inner knowing, good judgment, or knowledge that reflects a certain morality, or understanding of right and wrong. An example of the moral wisdom that Walker gleans from her mother's story is the necessity for her mother to have compassion on the white woman, realize the ways in which jealousy tormented her, and move to a place of forgiveness and letting go.

She writes, "When I listen to my mother tell and retell this story I find that the white woman's vindictiveness is less important than Aunt Mandy's resourceful generosity or my mother's ready stand of corn."[30] In this passage, Walker points to the moral wisdom of placing less emphasis on the "white woman's vindictiveness" in the story and more on the fact that her mother was able to quickly move past the woman's racism to find resources to create wholeness for her and her family. Relying on her "ready stand of corn" and "Aunt Mandy's resourceful generosity" prove to be the elements that enable her mother to tune into her own agency in the situation and change the direction of the experience. In essence, the moral wisdom that emerges from the story is that it is more important to find ways of survival by leaning on one's own resourcefulness and the resourcefulness of community than it is to hold on to bitterness and anger. While anger at the injustice of the situation is an important aspect in the story and one that Walker implies ought to be expressed, in the final analysis, she makes clear that it is not Mrs. Walker's anger that puts food on the table. Rather, it is her amazing resourcefulness, ability to move on, and letting go for the sake of survival that feed the family.[31]

The moral wisdom that emerges from the story is reflective of several values, including, being resourceful in spite of oppression, self-reliance, communal interdependence, and letting go for the sake of survival.[32] Embodying this moral wisdom so that it impacts the everyday actions and decisions of women and their communities leads to reflection on a fifth step—taking action upon the wisdom and values learned from black women's stories.

Step Five: Taking Action upon the Wisdom and Values

The fifth step that can be seen in Walker's method is to act upon the wisdom and values that are gleaned from black women's and black people's stories and experiences. Walker takes action against unjust systems of oppression through her activism as discussed in *Anything We Love Can Be Saved: A Writer's Activism.* In this book, Walker explains that her activism emerges from two important values that she learned from her mother, family, and the black community in which she was raised.

> Activism is often my muse...it is organic. Grounded in my mother's love of beauty, the well-tended garden and the carefully swept yard, her satisfaction in knowing everyone in her environment was sheltered and fed.[33]

Recalling how she shares her mother's desire to see the fullness of humanity honored in each child in their community, whatever their circumstances and background, Walker reveals that she values the goodness of humanity and tries to promote wholeness in individuals and communities while creating safe spaces for persons living into the fullness of themselves in her environment. It is important to note that Walker describes her activism as being rooted in her "love of nature and [her] love of human beings."[34] Trust in both the goodness of humanity and the uniqueness, versatility, nurturing, and giving spirit of nature should be part of one's ethical system. The interconnection of these values is reflected for Walker in the religious tradition of Earth-spirituality, or, as she calls it in this essay, paganism. Noting the changes and transformations and the ebbs and flows in her religious journey in this 1995 piece, Walker describes her Earth-orientation saying:

> In day-to-day life, I worship the Earth as God—representing everything—and Nature as its spirit.... "Pagan" means "of the land, country dweller, peasant"....It also means a person whose primary spiritual relationship is with Nature and the Earth.[35]

Valuing the Earth is a central tenet for Walker's ethics, and this ethical imperative is interwoven in much of her ethical decision making regarding other ethical issues. Though detailed discussion on Walker's ecospirituality and the basis for her ecowomanist thought lies beyond the scope of this work, it is important to mention that further explanation of Walker's ethics concerning nature offers key entry points for environmental ethics and provides an opening to work on ecowomanist perspective.

The act of living out these values as exemplified iin Walker's activism is an important model for womanist religious thought, for it suggests that beyond the ivory towers of academic discourse, true womanist spirituality is lived out among the people and within the self as movements of empowerment and action. Step five, to act upon wisdom and values ascertained from black women's and black people's stories and experiences, is an important step to honor in Walker's approach to ethics because it helps chart a path for womanist ethics to notice its interconnection with the Earth.[36]

Step Six: Use Empowerment Gained from the Action to Move toward Justice

In a move familiar to feminist and womanist ethical paradigms, the final step that can be observed from Walker's approach to ethical dilemmas is praxis oriented. The sixth step urges readers to become activists by using the empowerment established from steps four and five to create and secure a passion for justice for the Earth, the practice of Earth-honoring faith tradition, and ethics that value the full humanity of all people and earthlings. This step not only emphasizes the importance of individual activism as in step five but also advances urgency for communal activism. One essay that illustrates step six in Walker's approach is "Nuclear Madness: What You Can Do?" In this review of Helen Caldicott's book *Nuclear Madness,* Walker supports Caldicott's thesis and further directs the reader to get involved in antinuclear activism.

> What can we do? . . . I do not believe we should waste any time looking for help from our legal system. Nor do I have faith in politicians, scientists, or "experts." I have great faith in people. . . . As individuals we must join others. . . . Talk to your family; organize your friends. Educate anybody you can get your mouth on. Raise money. Support those who go to jail. Write letters to those senators and congressmen who are making it easy for the nuclear-power industry to kill us.[37]

By establishing community activism as a goal and Earth justice as central for her ethics, Walker's sixth step connects theoretical understandings of justice to the practical achievement and living out of justice. In this particular example, it is not just the wisdom and values gleaned from black women and black people that Walker acts upon but also the basic knowing that if the Earth is to survive, humans must honor her.

Explication of the six steps that Walker uses to approach ethical issues and of the values that can be gleaned from her mother's story are helpful in supporting my thesis that argues that uncovering Walker's ethical voice and perspective reveals a powerful resource for womanist ethics. In addition, these six values are helpful in providing a frame for a womanist virtue ethic.

A Womanist Virtue Ethic

A womanist virtue ethic is a set of canonical virtues and values that reflects certain dispositions and habitual practices of women of African descent who model appropriate and ethical behavior in their communities. Virtues can be described as habitually practiced characteristics of a person or the process of developing good habits of character so that they are a normal part of one's way of being in the world. Values are the standards and principles by which we judge worth or preference. Together, virtues and values are used as measuring codes by which to evaluate ethical or moral action and behavior. As mentioned above, there is an interconnection between virtues and values in that virtues often are reflective of the values that are most pronounced in a community. Thus, virtues based on the prominence of these values become standards of ethical action and being. Promoting wholeness and well-being in the overall community is as important as promoting wholeness and well-being in the individual.

Similar to the virtue theories that have the influence of an Aristotelian approach to ethics, a womanist virtue ethic is teleological in nature, focusing on the primary moral goal of good community including accountability and responsibility, when confronting an ethical dilemma or making an ethical decision. The set of virtues and values takes into account the goal of community well-being and thriving in African Diasporic life, as well as the necessity of survival. In doing so, the womanist virtue ethic honors a mode of constant resistance to multiple forms of oppression in pursuit of its overarching moral goals of wholeness and good community.

Virtue ethics is a Western form of thought influenced by Aristotle that essentially judges a person's character according to a specific set of religious or moral virtues.[38] A set of these moral virtues helps develop an ethical standard of behavior and disposition. Whereas decision-ist approaches to ethics focus on a person's conduct and help people decide what is a right or wrong thing to do, which choices and actions should be made, and what moral norms and values are important to maintain in order to live the "good life," virtue ethical approaches are designed to focus on a person's character, emphasizing character development and moral disposition. Instead of asking the question "what ought we to do?" familiar to decisionist approaches, virtue ethical approaches ask questions such as "how well does the person's character match the virtues upheld by the community?" "what are the character traits or virtues that guide a person's ethical perspective and behavior?" and "how and in what environment were those virtues shaped?" Concerning Aristotle's particular inductive approach (versus Plato's deductive analysis), which regards cultural influences as important when examining the virtues practiced in a particular community, the question, "what cultural circumstances impact the development of ethical or unethical behavior?" also arises as crucial for ethical inquiry.

The last question mentioned above is imperative for womanist virtue ethical approaches. Rather than following a preestablished set of norms and values often heavily influenced by the dominant culture, womanist virtue ethical approaches consider how cultural circumstances inform the situation. They lift up the cultural environment and circumstances that can influence individual and communal ethical perspectives, and influence particular values such as survival, as a result of dealing with systematic oppressions, including, racism, classism, sexism, heterosexism, homophobia, and environmental injustice. The approach is multipurpose in that it simultaneously uncovers the stories, experiences, moral codes, virtues, and values of women of African descent while validating these sources of women's voices and theological and ethical perspectives as epistemologies worthy of exploration and ethical inquiry. This kind of womanist ethical approach lends itself to theological ethical, social ethical, moral biographical, and interdisciplinary methods in order to analyze how layered internal and external oppressions can result in violence, rape, and systems of self-hate and address how agency-producing ethical solutions can reform individual moral choice and ethical conduct. The virtues, values, and moral wisdom gleaned from the writings of Alice Walker, including, wholeness, uncovering and validating voices and stories of women of African descent, survival and liberation, honoring women's sexualities and the act of self-naming, good community, mutuality in relationship (communal interdependence), communal sufficiency, being resourceful in spite of oppression, self-reliance, and letting go for the sake of survival help chart ethical guides and pathways for life. Together they form a web-like interdependent structure that frames a womanist virtue ethic.

5

Take Back Your Life: Virtues to Live By

Laughing out loud, joking about odd family characteristics, and finding out how family recipes came to the kitchen table in the first place are traditions generally associated with African and African American family culture. However, when it comes to discussing how trauma, violence, and abuse can impact family dynamics, a silence often weaves its way into family histories. African American family culture does not always allow for open conversation about the painful legacy of slavery, the sorrow that accompanies oppression, or the suffering that can be caused by intracommunal and family abuse. While religious settings, healing services, and faith communities can serve as safe places where stories of trauma can be released, silences can be broken, and survivors find the right and courage to come to voice, "family secrets" are often hushed in the home. In an attempt to save the next generation from having to endure the pain of these secrets, often elders in the community or people in the family make a decision *not* to tell. Echoing Audre Lorde's sentiment, "your silence will not protect you,"[1] Alice Walker's essays, short stories, and novels provide examples of uncovering family secrets and spilling truths about African American communities. Claiming that ignoring, hiding, or repressing the pain of trauma suffered by so many survivors in the community is an ineffective strategy and serves only to further harm, Walker's writings "rip off the scab," so to speak, of collective memories of violence, pain, and trauma.

The uncovering of rape, domestic violence, incest, and racially induced violence in Walker's essays is often taken from the shared accounts and stories of survival intertwined with African American history. Regarding her decision to uncover the painful legacy of domestic violence and incest in *The Color Purple,* she explains the necessity she felt to write and raise awareness about the need for healing and wholeness in and among African American communities: "Ever since I was a child, I had been aware of the high rate of domestic violence in our town, among our people; wives shot or stabbed to death, children sometimes abused and beaten."[2] Describing how in some cases the violence in African American families and communities can be linked to the legacy of slavery, Walker's writings explain that violent and oppressive treatment of slaves by slaveholders was sometimes internalized by the slaves themselves and passed on as methods of discipline, rebuke, and punishment. This practice of violence did not break at the same time the chains of slavery did. Rather, even as black and African slaves became free women and men, the death-dealing effects of slavery became cloaked in various forms of intracommunal and intimate violence and used as tools of self-hatred. Although many African American women and men claimed freedom, they were not really free at all. In many cases, violence was used as an outlet for anger about societal oppressions like racism and classism, and intimate violence between friends became a way of reestablishing control and power in a world that did not honor the agency of black people.

In an effort to peel back the layers of silence incurred over time, Walker engages the issues of rape and domestic violence directly in *The Color Purple*. As discussed above, the book details the life and coming-to-age story of a young girl/woman named Celie. Dark-skinned and considered unattractive by her family, Celie is abused as a child by her step-father and then forced into an abusive marriage. The story follows Celie's harrowing journey of survival as she endures the role of servant/slave to her husband and caregiver to several of his children and his mistress, Shug Avery. In the book, Celie's life intersects with the lives of other African American women, also struggling to survive the multiple oppressions of racism, classism, sexism, and in some cases homophobia. It is through admiring, loving, and attending to another woman, Shug, that she comes to accept her sexual identity as a part of herself and to see her own beauty.

Moving through another self-actualizing "birthing" process, Celie is betrayed by Shug. Though heartbroken, Celie learns to pick up the pieces of her own life and heart to reengage the courage that she has exhibited her entire life in order to come to voice and take back her power. Using her newfound agency to build emotional, spiritual, and financial stability, Celie gives herself permission to follow her passion as a seamstress and shopkeeper in a way that builds community around her. Now, clear of her own identity and accomplished as an entrepreneur, her children, once taken from her, are returned to her in part due to the repentant effort of one of the people who abused her trust and innocence Mr._____. By the end of the story, Celie has learned to take back her life, engage her own power, come to voice, and use her own agency to fight for her bodily and sexual rights and to resist anything that would hinder freedom and wholeness for her body, mind, and soul. In her movement through pain and suffering to courage and self-determination she reaches a place of self-respect, self-naming, and self-knowledge. Celie learns to love herself by finding courage in her own ability to survive and is able to encourage and celebrate the survival stories of other women and the community around her. Celie overcomes abuse in the story and finds an indomitable courage to live life to the fullest while strengthening her own and her community's commitment to wholeness. These two points serve as the primary inspiration for the book.

Despite being honored with the Pulitzer Prize, Walker's novel received venomous attacks by critics. Many African American literary critics harshly charged Walker with uncovering an intracommunal issue, "airing dirty laundry," and unjustly calling attention to domestic violence and sexist brutality. The book was charged with igniting tensions between African American men and African American women and striking a loud chord within the hearts of African American women who shared memories of having suffered abuse at the hands of women and men. Walker was accused of portraying African American men (and some women) in the book as those who used their fists and vicious tongues to beat out their own frustrations with oppression onto the heads, hearts, and bodies of African American women. Shocked by the depth of denial that many African Americans were displaying, Walker recalls her deep disappointment and profound dismay that African American communities were not willing to admit to the injustices and forms of violence that were taking place in the lives and livelihoods of women in their own communities.

Walker speaks significantly about her understanding of why particular critics responded so negatively in *The Same River Twice: Honoring the Difficult, A Meditation on Life, Spirit, Art and the Making of the Film The Color Purple Ten Years Later*. In the work, Walker writes that the reason she believes that both African American men and women critics pounced on her work was because it let out a secret—the secret of sexist brutality, domestic violence, and intracommunal abuse in African American communities. Walker's writing of *The Color Purple* as well as her support and role in the production of the film are prime examples of how Walker's social protest voice hits the page and the screen.

Just as the social protest style in her novel results in the telling of African American women's stories for the sake of uncovering lessons of survival, so too does Walker suggest strategies of resistance helpful for women living in the present day in her essays. She examines the stories of women to mine the wisdom of their lives that can encourage and increase the likelihood of survival and thriving among present-day African American women. This fact is evidenced in no greater place than her essay "In Search of Our Mothers' Gardens." Here, she not only uncovers the stories of prominent black literary figures such as Phillis Wheatley, but also celebrates the stories of unnamed and less known black women, including her own mother, as we have analyzed in the previous chapter.

"In Search of Our Mothers' Gardens" is an award-winning essay, written in 1974, that brilliantly articulates the power of black women's stories, artistry, and creativity. In it, Walker lifts up the importance of remembering black women's stories that have been historically devalued. The essay opens with a scene from Jean Toomer's book *Cane*, through which Walker brings to light an innate spirituality embodied by black women. Despite the abuses and oppressions black women have historically faced and continue to face, the innate and natural *spirit* within black women, Walker argues, blooms into passion and strength for life. While society paints a picture of black women as sexual objects and "mules of the world," Walker uncovers an image of black women as creative artists and intellectuals. By connecting themselves to their own innate spirit, these artists become divine artists, creators of beauty, and survivors by strength.

Drawing a comparison between black women of today and black women who lived during the slavery and postslavery era, Walker names the latter women (whose innate spirituality helped them to survive) as grandmothers and mothers of black women living in the present day. "These grandmothers and mothers of ours were…artists; driven to a numb and bleeding madness by the springs of creativity in them for which there was no release. They were Creators, who lived lives of spiritual waste, because they were so rich in spirituality—which is the basis of Art."[3] Representing black women as artists instead of simply "mules of the world," Walker resets the historical contexts in which black grandmothers and mothers lived in order to recover and re-present their stories accurately. One way in which Walker recasts the images of black women in the essay is by highlighting black women artists such as Nina Simone, Roberta Flack, and Aretha Franklin, who have told their stories of survival through song. In a style familiar to black women artists, Walker connects the power of these songs and voices to the expressed literary voice of Phillis Wheatley. Recasting the image of Wheatley from a black slave girl riddled with self-hate into a formative figure for the black women's literary movement, Walker explains that Wheatley was not an "idiot or a traitor...a sickly little black girl, snatched from [her] home and country and made a slave; [she was] a woman who still struggled to sing the song that was [her] gift, although in a land of barbarians who praised [her] for [her] bewildered tongue." Addressing the ancestral spirit of Phillis Wheatley directly, Walker writes, "It is not so much *what* you sang, as that you kept alive, in so many of our ancestors, the notion of song."[4] In addition to lifting the experience and story of Phillis Wheatley, Walker validates the importance of black women's experiences by naming the stories from her own mother as a source for black women's spirituality, creativity, and artistry. Wondering out loud about whether the artistry of black women who were not as well known as Wheatley, Nella Larsen, Frances Harper, or Zora Neale Hurston was ever expressed, Walker explains that retelling black women's stories, such as her mother's, helps to validate and unearth stories of unknown mothers, which can provide links and pathways of survival for black women living in the present. Connecting her mother's artistry, shown through her storytelling and planting of flower gardens, to the artistry expressed by black women writers, Walker suggests that the act of uncovering black women's stories validates black women's experiences as real and empowering. For the womanist ethicist surveying Walker's collection of essays and prose, it is clear how her writings provide resources, values, and virtues helpful in charting a path for ethical living.[5]

Virtues to Live By

Attention has already been given to a set of values that can be lifted from analysis of Walker's essays. I now turn to a focus on seven virtues gleaned from her work that provide an inner core to the womanist virtue ethic. A virtue is a disposition or characteristic habitually developed over time in the individual and in the community that marks good moral character and reflects certain basic values, such as wholeness and good community. Often these virtues reflect the values that contribute to a common moral discourse embedded in cultural groups, such as peoples of African descent. Acknowledgment of and respect for the full humanity of persons and beings, justice, the pursuit of quality of life, and honoring the full agency of women of African descent and their communities are some of the goals and manifestations of living into a set of womanist virtues, or embodying a womanist virtue ethic.

Certain virtues practiced habitually through everyday actions and behaviors influence the way ethical decisions are made. Often, in keeping with an African cosmological perspective wherein the spiritual presence of ancestors, God, nature, and humanity are linked, womanist virtues exemplify basic values held by the person and the community as a way of promoting the interdependence between the realms of spirit, history, and nature, and in turn, justice, wholeness, and good community for women and all Creation living with the Earth.[6]

Seven Virtues

In this section, I highlight seven virtues that I gleaned from the analysis of Walker's writings discussed in this book. They are generosity, graciousness, compassion, spiritual wisdom, audacious courage, justice, and good community. These virtues are the key components of womanist virtue ethic. Analysis of Walker underscores that these virtues are habitually practiced by women of African descent and are worthy of being passed on to women living in the present day. In order to best highlight the virtues, I have explained their opposites, vices. The seven vices that are described are greed, unkindness, arrogance, foolhardiness, cowardice, injustice, and lack of accountability in community[7].

Virtue: Generosity

The virtue of generosity is illustrated in Walker's recounting of her mother's stories, which show both her mother's generous nature in providing education and safe space for community children and her Aunt Mandy's willingness and foresight to have and share resources with her family to help them survive the winter. Generosity can be described as a deep willingness to give help, assistance, time, and money freely with no ulterior motive. This virtue is often portrayed as paramount in African Diasporic moral communal life, in part because of the oppressive context in which peoples of African descent have had to live. Sticking together in order to survive and resist multiple oppressions is itself a strategy to overcoming oppression. This experience of having to lean on and to depend on one another promotes the value of communal sufficiency. At the same time, however, generosity as it is understood in many African Diasporic communities is shared beyond this intraracial or cultural community and practiced across racial, cultural, and creation lines. One example of this is in Walker's writings about the connection between peoples of color and the Earth. In essays including "Only Justice Can Stop a Curse,"[8] Walker reflects on the intimate connection sharecroppers had with the Earth and the common value of generosity practiced by sharecroppers and observed in the giving nature of the Earth. Honoring the generous way of being of the Earth, Walker implies that this value of generosity functions in a constant cycle of cherishing, providing, receiving, and giving.

In contrast to generosity, greed is a vice that suggests an overwhelming want or desire to have more than one actually needs. Greed refers to an unsatisfying, insatiable desire for something that often takes away from the balance of others' having enough, be it power, money, acclaim, or attention. That is to say, greed often feeds into the crooked notion that creating an imbalance in resources or crippling someone else's chance to have by acts of violence or abuse can be justified. To be more specific, taking more than one can use is an example of greed. In a consumerist culture such as the one that exists in the North American context wherein media images, popular trends, and the illusion of economic security promote an unbalanced desire for things beyond one's means and a constant sense of unsatisfaction, greed produces a stream of economic debt and personal doubt. Rebuking any sense of moderation, greed rejects any sense of fairness or mutuality and cuts into communal ways of sharing in order to promote crude individualism by any means necessary.

Virtue: Graciousness

Graciousness is often recounted in Walker's writings as an attitude that black women display in order to support subversive ways of coming to voice. It creates space wherein women maintain their own dignity in the midst of chaos and remind themselves of their own agency and power, in spite of the oppression or violence they face. Though being gracious operates as an outer display of dignity, there is an inner nature of the virtue of graciousness that is revealed in Walker's portrayal of her mother's kindness, creativity, and artistic strength. Creating room for others to come into their own voice through listening, being fully present and forgiving another human being based on a practice of extending grace to all creatures, simply because they are creatures sharing a common Earth, are also elements that reflect the graciousness that Walker enters into words. Turning to her reflections about Zora Neale Hurston, Walker often remarks upon the boldness of Hurston's personality as well as the gracious way that she entered the anthropological study of black folk culture. Noting the importance of respect and trust embedded in Hurston's anthropological method of humbly asking for and then accepting an invitation to conduct work and record stories, Walker illustrates graciousness as a central point for Hurston's method and her approach to honoring trust to uncover black people's and black women's stories.

The virtue of grace has been lifted in dialogue among womanist ethicists before. "Quiet grace" is a moral characteristic of black women named by Katie G. Cannon. In her book *Black Womanist Ethics*, Cannon describes moral characteristics and practices of black women that are in keeping with their moral life and conduct. In this work, I name those characteristics virtues. In relation to "quiet grace," Cannon explains that the qualifying word "quiet" refers to the "invisibility of their [black women's] moral character." Noting how moral agency has never been assumed to belong to black women historically from the dominant perspective, Cannon describes black women's graceful ways of creating "something where there was nothing before" without recognition. "Most of the time this is done without the mumble of a single word, without an eruptive cry to the hierarchal systems that oppress her."[9] Providing several examples of how black women protagonists and other characters throughout Zora Neale Hurston's novels display grace, Cannon shows how the moral characteristic of grace is revealed in human interactions with one another and through a divine interaction with God.

Graciousness can be described as an act full of kindness, tact, and politeness, displaying grace, mercy, and compassion. The opposite side of this is the vice of unkindness, being unmerciful, pushing one beyond their limits so as to provoke them on purpose, or intentionally (and sometimes unconsciously), causing harm. Noting how white supremacist notions helped to legalize dehumanizing acts against peoples of African descent in the United States, Walker's writings suggest that the roots of abuse and oppressive systems lie in unkindness, harshness, and attitudes of dominon and control. These perspectives illustrate the opposite of graciousness, the vice of unkindness. At the root of this vice is the logic of domination and the attitude of hierarchal control. The logic of domination describes a way of thinking that supports value-hierarchal thinking, and concepts of power that suggest that one must take power from another in order to have it, rather than to envisioning power as something shared. Concepts of priviledge are also founded on the logic of domination as they consider one person, group, or being as having innate superiority over another, thus justifying any act of violence or control over the other. In contrast to graciousness in which each person's and every creature's being is honored as an interconnected part of Creation, the vice of unkindness acts without regard to another person's worth, body right (a person's right to use and move their bodies as they choose to; also, one's autonomy especially regarding the agency they have over their own body), or being.[10] It sets the groundwork for policies that privilege some over others, and perpetuates systems of injustice that are not in keeping with a virtue in which grace is given, lived into, and received.

Virtue: Compassion

Compassion is a unique virtue that refers to a deep knowing and alert awareness of the suffering of another, accompanied by an action to alleviate it. Having compassion for the self is necessary when having compassion for others. This virtue is of primary importance for women, who are often bombarded with the stereotype and gender role of primary care giver though they may find it difficult to find time and space to take care of themselves as they are taking care of others. The wisdom that accompanies compassionate action includes attention to the self as the self is connected to community so that both are held in high esteem. As expressed in Peter J. Paris's concept of the interconnectedness between the self and the community and the understanding that both share the same primary moral goal of wholeness and good community, compassion is practiced for both the individual and the community.

Alice Walker expresses her thoughts on compassion in the closing lines of her essay "To Be Led by Happiness." Describing the "root of peace" that was planted into the ground as the basis of the nonviolent struggle of Martin Luther King Jr., the strong voice of Fannie Lou Hamer, and the simplicity of genius in Albert Einstein, Walker recalls the moments of being arrested during a protest for women and children of Iraq in Washington, DC: "We were women and children who loved ourselves in our Iraqi form of women and children; loving ourselves as humans meant loving ourselves as all humans. Connecting the experiences of women and children who were suffering across the world to the shared humanness of women and other protestors shouting for justice in Washington streets." Walker explains how living into compassion allows us to make connections to freedom and justice for all beings. She continues saying, "The heart enjoys experiencing the liberating feeling of compassion; it extends and glows, as if beaming its own sun upon the world."[11]

In contrast to compassion, selfishness does not open itself to mutual relationship or share the possibility of being aware of another person's suffering, because the self is preoccupied completely by the self. This vice rebukes in-depth knowing, or intimacy, cancels out spaces of empathy, and revolves around a gross arrogance and assumption that the individual's life and perspective are the only ones that matter. Negating knowledge that can be transformed into wisdom and cutting off opportunities to share or pass on critical life-affirming insights so needed in a world that is often overcome by violence, injustice, and misuse, the vice of cruelty or selfishness reveals just how necessary compassion is to the survival of humanity and the Earth.

Virtue: Spiritual Wisdom

Spiritual wisdom is knowledge and discernment that comes from a connection to Spirit and that can be used to guide one's ability to make decisions. This virtue is exemplified in the writings of Walker, particularly in her uncovering of the story of Rebecca Jackson, Shaker Eldress. In her book review of Jean Humez's collection of Jackson's writings, Walker describes the Spirit-led guidance that helped Jackson become a foremost religious figure in early nineteenth-century Christian history. Despite constant rebuttal from church leaders and parishioners in African Methodism and the refusal of the church to honor her quality of leadership and calling to preach the gospel according to the teachings of the Spirit, Jackson struck out on her own to find a denomination and religious community through which she could do the work of justice by aiding women and children in need. One of the few African American women of the nineteenth century whose religious life, theological reflections, and ethical decisions are recorded in print, Jackson's description of her faith to follow the "spirit within" both empowers women to listen to their own hearts and gives women courage to embrace the power of the Spirit within them.

Thomas Aquinas's writings about theological virtues shed light on a theological underpinning of the meaning of spiritual wisdom. His reflections on Pauline theological virtues such as faith, hope, love were separated from cardinal virtues, Platonic in origin (justice, temperance, fortitude, and prudence), to form an understanding of virtues as habits or dispositions "of the will towards a good end," seeded the source of virtue in God.[12] For Aquinas, the theological virtues of faith, hope, and love were infused into the moral or virtuous person by God's enabling them to "achieve supernatural ends...dependent on the action of God" and requiring them to "go beyond the norms set by natural virtue."[13] Thus, these theological virtues infused by the Spirit of God shaped human choice and action often toward the "good" for all from a divine perspective. Rather than philosophical knowledge being the sole base of virtue, Aquinas's theological virtues suggested that God and communion with God sparked a knowledge or wisdom that indeed shaped moral discourse.

Spiritual wisdom as a womanist virtue shares a like manner in that it carries a connection to a divine source of wisdom and knowledge that can shape one's ethical way of being. Often embodied within, the divine source of spiritual wisdom can be heard through black women's narratives about their own reasonings with the Spirit, their own interpretations of God's message, and their own reliance on a divine source of wisdom from within them to guide ethical decisions in everyday life. The evidence of spiritual wisdom can be described as a manifestation of a human's knowing that to be fully human is to be divine, following a concept introduced in the Gospel of Mary and other noncanonical texts wherein the true essence of humanity is Spirit.[14]

Arrogance, foolishness, rejection of divine leading, and lacking good sense that eventually leads to thoughtless action are examples of the opposite of spiritual wisdom. Arrogance can be described as "the incapacity to discern any source of wisdom beyond human reasoning."[15] Foolishness is often referred to as a vice particularly dangerous in African Diasporic life because of the frequently oppressive situational context that African peoples find themselves in. On top of having to resist multilayered oppressions, foolish thinking, foolish action, and foolish behavior may draw a person deeper into the calculated systemic patterns of dehumanization already lying in wait for them.

Virtue: Audacious Courage

Audacious courage is a virtue exemplified by many of the black women whose lives and stories are incorporated in Walker's prose. For example, Walker, noting the bold steps that Rebecca Jackson took, leaving her church, family, and home to pursue her understanding of sharing the gospel according to the Spirit's leading, Walker portrays courage as a womanist virtue. "Audacious" indicates the brave, often unexpected, and radical sense that grounds the courageous action frequently taken by women who believe strongly in their agency, their right to protect it, and the empowering justice necessary for establishing wholeness in community. Audacious courage as a womanist virtue also suggests a way of being in the world, that is, the ability to stand up and be counted, not only in word but also in deed.

In contrast, cowardliness suggests a lack of nerve to combat oppression and can be associated with fear. The vice of cowardliness is often based in a fear of knowing and accepting the self, and, in turn, in the fear of confronting and dismantling systems of oppression. Therefore, it does not offer a foundation for social and human transformation. Cowardliness can surface through acts of violence or aggression designed to place fear in someone else, often in an attempt to shift attention from the fears held by the person acting in violence. In contrast to audacious courage, cowardliness functions in an individualistic sphere instead of being a source for the community.

The virtue of courage can be found throughout womanist ethical scholarship, and most notably in *Black Womanist Ethics* where Cannon explicates an "unshouted courage": " 'Unshouted courage' is the quality of steadfastness, akin to fortitude, in the face of formidable oppression. The communal attitude is far more than 'grin and bear it.' Rather, it involves the ability to 'hold on to life' against major oppositions."[16] Noting the undeniable commitment to freedom and women's full assertion of their humanity, Cannon aligns her description of "unshouted courage" with an inner "conviction" for freedom that is alive with the richness of faith and perseverance in black life.

Virtue: Justice
Justice refers to fairness in relation to the self, others, and all life in Creation, and undergirds the drive toward social action that establishes equality, freedom, and human and environmental rights. Justice, also described as sound and reasonable judgment, is an overarching theme in womanist religious thought. Due to the social protest tradition of many womanist writers and protowomanist activists such as Sojourner Truth and Ida B. Wells, justice is central to any womanist perspective that takes seriously confronting oppressions such as racism, classism, sexism, homophobia, and environmental degradation. Justice is often described as the base of truth and balance for

a democratic society and celebrates the shared rights of all to have access to basic needs or goods, including water, shelter, education, and health care. The right to "home," to use a concept that emerges from Walker's writings, also includes justice claims for the right to access land and have a sense of belonging and place. While the ideology that supports land ownership and dominance over the land is considered unsacramental in many African indigenous and Native American traditions, the promotion of land and Earth rights as well as values that embrace Earth care are celebrated in the womanist virtue of justice.

According to womanist virtue, injustice is a vice. It occurs when a balance of fairness is upset by any social ill, systemic cultural production of evil, or individual act of violence rooted in any form of the logic of domination. Whether the injustice is a manifestation of external or internal forms of oppression, such as forms of internalized racism, sexism, classism, or homophobia (forms of self-hated), the results of trauma and abuse are generally symptoms that the vice of injustice is at work in society. Combating injustice through the habitual learning and practice of justice as a form of moral development is a crucial tenet in the work and scholarship of many womanist ethicists. This can be seen through the work of Katie G. Cannon, Emilie M. Townes, Marcia Y. Riggs, and Rosetta Ross. Justice holds primary significance in their work, actions, and living.

Justice is often defined in relationship to another womanist virtue— good community. For example, Emilie M. Townes writes in *In A Blaze of Glory: Womanist Spirituality As Social Witness*: "Justice holds us accountable to the demands of living in a community of responsibility and one that fosters self-worth and self-esteem for others and for itself."[17] Given the interconnectedness between the person and the community, justice serves as an instrument to bring about accountability in community and the practice of ethical responsibility.

Virtue: Good Community/Good Accountability

The promotion of community and the justice therein are said to be two of the highest moral goals for peoples of African descent.[18] However, clarity on the kind of community promoted is important to explain. Good community embodies a kind of accountability within the structure of the group that serves constantly to promote justice within and outside of the community. The reality of intracommunal violence and domestic partner violence within African American and African communities makes it imperative to recast descriptions of community to include a system of accountability. For an individual, being accountable means taking responsibility for one's failings, as well as one's contributions to mutual relationality, and finding ways to achieve a greater sense of balance between one's individual wants, needs, and desires and the wants, needs, and desires of others living into relationship with the Earth.

For me, living in good community includes living in mutual relationship with all forms of nature. The presence of self-centered anthropocentric attitudes reflective of power imbalance in relationship is one example of how connection in community can be assumed without emphasis on accountability. The historical and present-day realities of external and internalized forms of racism, classism, sexism, and homophobia are also towering signs of this. For communities, being accountable means holding one another and ourselves responsible to the interdependent web of life that holds us and connects us all together. The African proverb "I am because We Are" connotes the idea of good community and accountability in that it underscores the interconnectedness that we all share with each other.

Pointing communities in the right direction, toward developing into good, accountable, and sustainable communities, ethicist Emilie M. Townes writes the following:

> We have a responsibility for our future. We must decide if we are going to live in an uneasy, destructive, but comfortable acquiescence or in communal accountability.... so that we can see a God whose spirit calls us into a spirituality that loves our bodies into wholeness as God holds us in the palm of creation and with creation itself. We owe one another respect and the right to our dignity as people of God.[19]

Human mutuality, the ethical imperative to respond to the most marginalized, and the vivid and dynamic responsibility, ethicist Rosetta Ross argues, help with the formation and practice of good community and are essential parts of African American women activist stories during the civil rights movement. I contend that these frames for shaping good community were useful not only then but also now.

The lack of accountability in community can destroy the community. When people do not care enough for one another to hold them to standards that help to maintain wholeness and peace in a community, often invididuals in the community become fractured and damaged. Community serves to promote relationship and proper relationality between persons because it can reinforce fair treatment, proper engagement, and strategies for living that are condusive to such values as love, respect, and shared responsibility. Mutuality, a significant value expressed in the work of Alice Walker, as in the works of other feminist writers, is central to healthy relationship. When a community is present to support this value, all relationships are conducted in a reciprocal way. However, when there is a lack of accountability in the community so as to reinforce these values, then relationships themselves can become fractured, thus destroying the community.

* * *

As we have seen in the previous chapters, examining Walker's non-fiction work not only highlights her own voice and contributions as a resource for womanist ethics but also lifts important virtues and values practiced among and in the moral lives of women of African descent. When we return to interviews with Alice Walker noting her own dismay at the negative press and alarming reactions of readers and critics of *The Color Purple* who would have preferred discussion of intracommunal violence be kept silence we see how Walker's own work and the virtues that can be lifted from it promote a level of accountability within good community. Even as critics suggested that Walker's airing of dirty laudry regarding the realities of incest, and violence against women was too risky and inappropriate, it is Walker's own commitment to maintaining wholeness in community that pushes her onward to uncover injustice and reveal places where the community is fractured and in need of healing. Her move can be considered an incarnation of the virtues named above, for a community cannot thrive when there is hidden violence in it that mimics the violence that has been done to it. Using grace and audacious courage in her writing style, Walker not only lifts these and other virtues as important to the black community, but also lives into them herself. As literary scholar Carolyn Medine puts it, "Walker's writing style practices what she preaches."[20] Whether leading movements in social change, human transformation, and justice, surviving acts of trauma, parenting, or practicing values in everyday life, these womanist virtues and values gleaned from the work of Alice Walker provide a roadmap for living a moral life in the present day.

6

Third-Wave Womanism: Expanding Womanist Discourse, Making Room for Our Children

As womanist theology and ethics celebrate almost thirty years in the academy, it is important to lift up the valuable contributions womanists and nonwomanists alike have made toward the development of the interreligious, global-reaching, and interdisciplinary field of womanist religious thought. Acknowledging the various streams of womanism that flow from the North American context and the appropriation of Walker's term "womanist," as well as the streams of thought emerging from African and Africana literary movements, this chapter reviews various understandings of the womanist movement as a whole. It also proposes an expansion of womanist discourse and introduces a third wave of womanist religious thought. Some of the hallmarks of this wave include expanding the interreligious landscape of womanist religious thought, focusing on the global links within the field, and taking special note of the connections between African and African American womanist literary and scholarly writers, thus encouraging interdisciplinary study in order to expand the traditional boundaries of the field.

Waves in Womanist Thought

The term "wave" is often used in theoretical discourse to describe a shift in focus or to distinguish one group of scholars in a certain field from a different group of scholars working in the same field. In feminist discourse, for example, the term "waves," used over and above the expression "generations," suggests a fluid motion between varying theological perspectives, ideological and philosophical ideas, and different experiential entry points into the movement, rather than the more static and constructed connotation of "generations." In the womanist context, the latter word can be interpreted as divisive and not in keeping with the reality of the intergenerational dialogue and exchange experienced in womanist circles. I argue that "waves" be used to describe different perspectives ebbing and flowing but all alive in womanist thought. I believe "waves" is also in keeping with the key intergenerational mentoring and dialogue that occur in womanist discourse.

Still, a cautionary note is helpful in determining just what is means when we use the term "wave"—for as Susan Shaw and Janet Lee, scholars in Women's Studies, have discovered, even the meaning and use of the wave metaphor are shifting in academic discourse. Malinda A. Berry observes that the language of waves in feminist thought can suggest a form of periodization that is helpful in "delineating water-shed moments in the women's movement for freedom";[1] however, of late, there has been a growing shift in the way the term "wave" is used and interpreted. Increasingly, how one refers to herself as a first, second, third, or fourth waver depends less upon a description of a time period and more upon how she personally identifies with cer-tain "philosophical ideas of feminism."[2] Building upon the work of Shaw and Lee, Berry further observes that "over time an ideological entrenchment has come to define each wave rather than the historical moments that shaped the varied responses of feminist-oriented activ-ists, scholars, and organizers."[3] Shaw and Lee describe this shift in an introductory textbook essay, "What Does Women's Studies Have to Do with Feminism?":

> Despite the advantages of using a "wave metaphor" to characterize the developments in feminism, the metaphor distracts attention from the continuity of feminist activity and runs the risk of setting up dis-tinctions and potential intergenerational divisiveness between a more stodgy, second wave generation, devoid of sexuality and unwilling to share power, and a younger, self-absorbed generation obsessed with popular culture and uncritically sexualized. Neither of these extremes reflects reality; it is enough to say that just as feminism encompasses diversity, so feminists do not all agree on what equality looks like or how to get there.[4]

I believe this conversation in feminist thought can serve womanist religious thought, for in a similar vein, there are various interpreta-tions of waves and generations swirling about in womanist discourse, and clarity on this will help move us forward.[5] I argue that the wave metaphor and image of water are still helpful in understanding the various modes, methods, and ideologies alive in womanist thought and, as such, actually facilitate the continuity among forms of womanist activism and scholarship in a way that the categorical term "generation" does not. Adopting the wave metaphor in womanist language, I think, is a good choice, and there are certain realities that, while not all positive, currently protect us from the risk identified by Shaw and Lee above. These realities include the tradition of engaging and nurturing womanist intellectual community and the commitment to both womanist mentoring (sometimes intergenerational) and womanist accountability. The latter entails a network of systems, ideally based on positive and healthy cultural relationships between women of African descent designed to "check a sistah" and ensure that every woman is walking in the way of justice and honoring the divine in herself, the Earth, her sisters, and others. In this regard, womanist work is not a job, a career choice, or an attitude. It is a way of being.

Thus, the language of and delineations between waves and generations of feminist work are helpful in the discourse of womanist religious thought. Rather than separating scholars and scholarship into various generations, it is more helpful, I think, to imagine us moving as a river toward full liberation and wholeness for women across the globe and in particular for women of the African Diaspora.

There have been several attempts to distinguish one group of womanists from another that are worth noting. One of the first attempts to do so is found in the article "Roundtable Discussion: Christian Ethics and Theology in Womanist Perspective," authored by Cheryl J. Sanders, with responses by Katie Cannon, Emilie Townes, Shawn Copeland, bell hooks, and Cheryl Townsend Gilkes.[6] Another version of this kind of roundtable discussion attempting to decipher various camps or perspectives within womanist religious thought appeared in the *Journal of Feminist Studies in Religion* seventeen years later. Authored by Monica A. Coleman, with responses from Katie Cannon, Arisika Rasak, Irene Monroe, Debra Mubashshir Majeed, Lee Miena Sky, Stephanie Mitchem, and Traci West, "Roundtable Discussion: Must I Be a Womanist?"[7] revealed some of the emerging womanist perspectives and raised questions about the origins of womanist method and thought. Still a third attempt to distinguish between womanist groups, and in this case generations, comes from Stacey Floyd-Thomas's introduction to *Deeper*

Shades of Purple: Womanism in Religion and Society, wherein she makes a clear mark between the movement of womanism and the writings and activism of Alice Walker. She claims that apart from Walker and her definition of the term, womanism began as a movement among African American women religious scholars as a way of charting their own path through the dangerous terrain of the academy and setting African American women's voices and experiences as instrumental reflection points for theology, biblical studies, and ethics. She writes, "Though the term womanist was coined by Walker, womanism became a movement when black women scholars of religion used their logos—marked by their intellectual reason and God-given sense—to reconcile theoretical/theological reflection to social transformation which would forever change the way they constructed knowledge and the way knowledge constructed them."[8] She states that womanism as a movement really began in 1985 with the bold act of several black women scholars claiming space at the American Academy of Religion and Society of Biblical Literature annual meeting. While I acknowledge and honor the boldness and bravery of these women, I disagree with Floyd-Thomas's assumption that this is the only place where the movement of womanism began.[9] In fact, it can be argued to have begun before 1985 and in a number of different scholarly disciplines and activist communities that also embodied a trust and commitment to women's wholeness and liberation from multiple oppressions.

The Womanist Reader, edited by Layli Phillips, is helpful in developing this point. A quick review of the book reveals just how many different disciplines beyond theology, biblical studies, and ethics have been touched and emerged from Walker's definition of "womanist." Citing sources from Walker's nonfiction work, African women's literature, feminist reflections on womanist thought, and the fields of history, visual arts, theater and film studies, communication and media studies, as well as psychology, anthropology, education, social work, nursing studies, sexuality studies, and architecture, Phillips's text shows just how varied and interdisciplinary womanist work is, and just how widely womanist methods, practices, and approaches are used. The womanist movement is not local to just the North American context; it is a global movement. Perhaps the most engaging proof of this fact is that there are three mothers to the word "womanist."

According to Phillips, the coinage and meaning of the term "womanist" was also being discussed by two other women of

African descent and working as literary scholars around the time that Walker defined the term. Chikwenye Okonjo Ogunyemi, a Nigerian writer, and Clenora Hudson-Weems, an African American Africana Studies scholar, also began using the terms "African womanism" and "Africana womanism" in the late 1970s and early 1980s. Ogunyemi describes "African Womanist" in her work *Africa Wo/Man Palava: The Nigerian Novel by Women* and in various articles. In the book, she writes about the shared sources of feminism and particularly feminist literary thought that helped to form a literary movement among Nigerian women writers. While it was difficult for African women writers who carried any notion of feminist ideology in their work to get published (more often than not it was almost impossible to achieve this feat), some African women broke through the heavily patriarchal African literary context to publish novels. In her own work, Ogunyemi credits such women writers as Ifeoma Okoye, Flora Nwapa, Adaora Lily Ulasi, and Buchi Emecheta for achieving the seemingly impossible as she found strategies to write women's counternarratives in African literary thought and overcame ways in which feminism was considered to be "anti-African."[10] Though texts like Okoye's *Men without Ears* were often not well received by male critics, they are credited with shifting the tone in the African literary context and pushing women's voices and women's experiences to the forefront of the literary world.[11] In keeping with an African womanist literary movement, then, Ogunyemi argues that writing these remarkable stories and making them available for public consumption helps to prick the conscience of African peoples everywhere about the lives, struggles, and triumphs of women.

The work of Clenora Hudson-Weems and her coinage of "Africana womanism" also reveal a deep and abiding connection to the black women's autonomous activist tradition and such tenets as self-naming (*nommo*) also found within the frame of womanist religious thought. Emerging from an Africana paradigm, rather than being directly influenced by feminist or women's studies, Hudson-Weems's first book, *Africana Womanism: Reclaiming Ourselves,* features an in-depth study at eighteen characteristics and values present in the lives of Africana women that help them maintain their selves and their communities. Reading almost as a chart for an Africana womanist ethics, the characteristics include being a "self-namer, self-definer, family-centered, in concert with males in struggle, genuine in sisterhood, strong, whole, authentic, flexible role player, male compatible, respected, recognized, adaptable, respectful of elders, spiritual, ambitious, mothering and nurturing."[12] Recognizing these origins of the term "womanist" as influenced by the literary tradition (Alice Walker), Africana studies, (Clenora Hudson-Weems), and the African context (Chikwenye Okonjo Ogunyemi), I argue for an expansion of womanist religious thought that engages more global and interdisciplinary perspectives. This is not only accepting the reality of the global connection of women of African descent already present in the origins of womanist thought, but also suggests that the shared tradition of telling our stories exemplifies the task of uncovering women's stories as a major tenet in womanist scholarship.

Third-Wave Womanist Approaches

A word about my entry into the movement of womanism will help situate the third wave and my own contributions to womanist religious thought. As a third-wave womanist, I ground my understanding of the term "womanist" in the work of Alice Walker as well as the writings of other womanist writers, scholars in the academy, teachers, and activists who work for the betterment of the world and find connection with faith communities. While I, like other womanists, believe that Walker's definition of "womanist" holds particular significance for the work and methodologies used in womanist religious thought, I maintain that a focus on the definition alone is not enough for womanists to understand the depth of Walker's own ideas and contributions to womanist religious thought, whether locally or globally. I believe that to fulfill the task of womanist religious scholarship and uncover African and African American women's voices, stories, and theological and ethical perspectives, it is essential that we conduct serious study on Walker's work—nonfiction, fiction, prose, and poetry alike. Such comprehensive study will set the definition into context, thus providing a wider and deeper understanding of how "womanist" can be understood and used to shed light on African Diasporic women's religious expressions.

One of the hallmarks of third-wave womanism is to place emphasis on the global links within the body of womanism, thus highlighting the significance of theologies and religious perspectives that emerge from women of African descent as a way of expanding womanist discourse within and outside of theology, biblical studies, and ethics.

A second hallmark of third-wave womanist thought that results in the expansion of womanist religious thought is the acknowledgment of the religiously pluralistic perspectives embodied by African-descended women across the Diaspora who find their religious traditions life affirming and who also identify as womanists. Third, creating space for new interdisciplinary approaches and uncovering methodological connections between womanism and fields such as African womanist literary theory and African American literature and anthropology are also an important hallmark of the third wave. Other tasks important to third-wave womanist approaches include reexamining the appropriation, meaning, and interpretation of the term "womanist," as coined by Walker, especially in light of the origins of womanism, including African womanism and Africana womanism; clarifying the distinctions between waves in womanist religious thought; problematizing the traditional categories and language used in African American religious and womanist discourse; celebrating the origins of and differences and similarities between black feminist and womanist methods; and constructing new pedagogical styles and models of social activism that build upon the scholarship informed by the first two waves of womanist and black feminist religious thought.

Facing critiques such as (1) the necessity for womanist scholars to examine points of privilege, namely, economic privilege, that may be buried within the construction of womanism; (2) whether and how womanism can speak practically in order to contribute to discussion about globalization from its social location as a Western discourse in a first-world capitalist context; and (3) questions about the usefulness of the formulaic and perhaps hierarchal womanist "race-class-gender and heterosexist" ordered analysis initiates important conversations for womanists to take up in this third wave.

Expanding Womanist Religious Discourse: Making Global Links

One of the hallmarks of third-wave womanist religious thought is to give more attention to global links already present in womanist scholarship. This includes highlighting the significance of African women's theologies for womanist scholarship and uncovering methodological connections between African womanist literary theory and methods used by African American womanist scholars. There has already been mention of the three sources of womanist origins through the work of Alice Walker, Clenora Hudson-Weems, and Chikwenye Okonjo Ogunyemi. What makes this find so important is that it uncovers not only a global link between African American womanists and womanists from across the African Diaspora but also an interdisciplinary link infused in this Diasporic connection. That is, the mere fact that the term "womanist" has roots in both a North American and African continental context and is aided by interdisciplinary discourse suggests that the term itself and thus the movement speaks to the ideals of womanist thought (i.e., wholeness) in a variety of contexts throughout the globe. Womanist theology and ethics are not just for African American women, but rather this discovery points to the fact that womanist religious thought embodies a host of experiences, theo-ethical perspectives, and voices of women of African descent across the planet.

The point that three disciplines are represented in the origins of these three women scholars emphasizes the importance of interdisciplinary study for womanist religious scholarship and supports Cannon's move and method that honors black women's literature as a powerful resource for womanist theo-ethical reflection. It also suggests that there is a connection between these women, who represent different parts of the Diaspora.

In some cases, it is quite obvious where the interdisciplinary conversation can begin in order to link womanist religious theo-ethical questions with the work of Africana womanist literary theory. Hudson-Weems's book, *Africana Womanist Literary Theory*, discusses eighteen characteristics or values embodied and practiced by African women in order to promote the wholeness of communities and individuals. The values of community and wholeness are also well explicated in the work of several known womanist ethicists, including Cannon, Townes, Riggs, Ross, and Floyd-Thomas. Thus, there is an entry point of comparative work between the eighteen values and characteristics found in the work of Hudson-Weems and the values found in the work of the aforementioned ethicists.[13]

Beyond this, the work, activism, church leadership, and scholarship of many African women theologians, biblical scholars, and activists can also serve to inspire the whole of womanist religious thought.[14] For decades, African theologian Mercy Amba Oduyoye has been publishing work that has brought insight into the experience and theological perspectives of African women. Her work *Introducing African Women's Theology*[15] is one of the most comprehensive texts recording African women's Christian theological perspectives. One of the themes evident in Oduyoye's work that may serve as an entry point for womanist discourse is the relationship between culture and theology and, more specifically, the emphasis on enculturation within Christian theology within the development of African theology. As an author who has written from both a postcolonial, African women's, and feminist perspective, Oduyoye's insights on developing a meaning of human beingness that includes the fullness of women's identity and experience are a crucial part of a theological lens that develops themes of community, liberation, and fullness of being.[16]

Another theological concept in Oduyoye's work worth pursuing in conversation with North American womanists is the aspect of African cosmology and "Alafia" (well-being or wholeness of life and community). In light of the primary womanist value of wholeness identified in this study of Walker's nonfiction, this connecting point leaves room for additional discourse about how an African woman's theological sense of wholeness, as explicated in Oduyoye's work, connects, meshes, or coincides with a North American womanist sense of wholeness.

The words of African women theologians and religious thinkers published in *Women Healing Earth*[17] and *On Being Church: African Women's Voices and Visions*[18] also offer womanist religious thinkers, theologians, and ethicists in the North American context tremendous resources, especially regarding African women's religious connection to social activism and empowerment of women's relationship with the land and Earth. One of the activists who emerges as a model of social activism, whose work is worthy of exploration for ecowomanist perspectives, is Wangari Maathai. Author of *The Green Belt Movement: Sharing the Approach and the Experience* and *Unbowed*, Maathai's method of empowering African women with the resources, skill sets, and knowledge to replenish the Earth by planting trees across the country side is a novel grassroots approach of doing Earth activism that has global consequences.[19] Although Maathai does not reference African cosmology using theological and theo-ethical terms, it is important to acknowledge this influence in understanding the impact that planting trees and thus honoring the ancestors has on the accomplishments of the Green Belt Movement. Maathai's involvement in the environmental justice movement, as well as her books and her work illustrating the community-based organization model used in the Green Belt, has deep significance for methods in ecowomanist approaches involving an emphasis on womanist religious analysis and a push for environmental justice.

Expanding Womanist Religious Discourse: Interreligious Landscape, Interdisciplinary Approaches

Studying the various religions practiced by African-descended women who also claim the term "womanist" is not new. Several scholars, including Tracey Hucks, Dianne Stewart, Carole Dufrene, Debra Mubashshir Majeed, Arisika Rasak, and Linda A. Thomas[20] have been vocal for years about the need to break beyond the traditional Christian landscape of womanist theological inquiry and create room for womanist study of various religious practices.[21] Of special note is the connection that most of these scholars make between the need for multireligious study in womanist religious thought and the many women from across the African Diaspora whom womanism serves.[22] While opening womanist religious thought to be more theoretically constructive and more imaginative, Emilie Townes offers the "womanist dancing mind" as an image to uncover the need for womanist religious scholars in the North American context to be in better dialogue with African Diasporic women across the globe and welcome their voices and theological, religious, and ethical insights into the conversation. In her book *Womanist Ethics and the Cultural Production of Evil*, Townes writes about the necessity for womanist religious thought to expand her boundaries and make room for her children, pointing to the fact that scholars ought to identify and study all kinds of intersections that involve African Diasporic life and religion. In addition to investigating these relationships, Townes suggests, womanist religious work should become more interdisciplinary so that the various cultures of which we are a part and the art, religions, literature, and cultures that influence the thought and practice of African Diasporic religion in the lives of women throughout the Diaspora emerge in womanist discourse. She writes,

> The womanist dancing mind—the one that weaves in and out of Africa, the Caribbean, Brazil, the United States (South, North, East,

and West); the Christian, the Jewish, the Muslim, the, *Candomble,* the Santeria, the Vodun, the Native American, the caste of color, the sexuality, the sexual orientation, the socioeconomic class, the age, the body image, the environment, the pedagogies, the academy—has before it an enormous intracommunal task. One in which we are trying to understand the assortments of African American life.[23]

Townes's invitation to expand womanist discourse is unique in that it points simultaneously to the models of interdisciplinary study already present and applied within womanist scholarship and to a new direction of furthering this kind of work. Referencing Cannon's interdisciplinary approach to womanist ethics, involving methodological tools from a sociohistorical perspective, and using African American women's literature as a resource, Townes signals how her own method is interdisciplinary. Building on a model of H. Richard Niebuhr's "responsibility ethics," centering a womanist scope of analysis, and adopting parts of a literary method established by Toni Morrison, Townes uses an interdisciplinary womanist method of scholarly engagement, a "conscience dialogue/interaction among the self, the community, and the society within a global culture" in order to fashion a new approach to womanist religious thought and womanist ethics.[24]

This innovative way of creating method so that the intricacies of African Diasporic religious life can come into view, I argue, is a primary foundation for the move toward establishing more interdisciplinary methods in womanist religious thought. One of the hallmarks of third-wave womanism is to be more inclusive of various religious perspectives held by women of African descent across the Diaspora; yet another looks at ways in which interdisciplinary approaches are needed to expand womanist religious thought and explore new boundaries; and I argue that Townes's work is a model out of which third-wave womanist approaches find grounding. It is from this place that these approaches connect with each other as a way of keeping womanist religious thought relevant in the midst of religiously pluralistic societies that help shape the practice and study of African Diasporic religious life. Building upon Townes's work, third-wave womanist approaches examine the ways in which many women of African descent combine aspects of a variety of religions to shape a spiritual path that empowers them to overcome oppressions. Here, the work of Jan Willis is helpful, and Akasha Hull observes that more and more women of African descent in the twenty-first century are embracing the notion of religious hybridity.[25]

> A new spirituality...is taking shape among many progressive African-American women at this turning of the twenty-first century. Arising around 1980...this spiritual expression builds on firm cultural foundations and traditional Christian religions, but also freely incorporates...[other religious] elements.[26]

The practice of combining, layering, or mixing and mashing elements of multiple religious traditions together to form one's spiritual path, guide one's religious values, and create a sense of wholeness in one's life may not be as new a phenomenon as Akasha Hull presumes in her 2001 book *Soul Talk: The New Spirituality of African American Women.* The concept and reality of spiritual hybridity, wherein multiple forms of religion are merged to provide a life orientation that honors the multiplicity of identity, connections to community, ancestral spiritual realm, and Earth existed long before the twenty-first century, especially in African American religious history and culture. I would contend that Hull's observation signals an acceptance of the interreligious spiritual fluidity already intrinsic to much of African American religious expression rather than a new practice in and of itself. In other words, what Hull names as a shift in African American women's spirituality, which often departs from a base religion like Christianity, is more in keeping with African American religious practice than one might think.

Basing his premise on the argument that African retentions can be traced through many rituals and practices evidenced in African and African American religious expression, historian Gayraud Wilmore explains that African American religion is hardly monolithic; it is rather fluid and complex. Multiple forms of religion often influenced by some aspect of African cosmology provide the foundation of the African Diasporic religious context. Recounting the history of African slaves carried from Africa to the New World beginning in 1607, Wilmore argues that the study of African American religious expression is less a study of a particular mode of Christianity that was adopted and adapted by certain slaves in the eighteenth and nineteenth centuries and more a study of the variety of intersections between religious practices, spiritual beliefs, and diverse understandings of divinity.

According to Wilmore, African slaves fused together a number of religious traditions as they came into the New World to orient themselves to a land where they were forced into slavery and to give meaning to their lives. He states,

> Well into the nineteenth century the slaves relied upon the most elemental presuppositions of a religious way of life to give consolation and meaning to their suffering. Whatever specific beliefs may have been salvaged from Africa, or from the breaking-in period in the Caribbean, they came under the most vigorous assault by the North American missionaries and plantation preachers. The polytheistic aspect of traditional African religion had to be surrendered under great duress despite the fact that the idea of a Supreme Being was not foreign to Africans. Yet the spirits of the ancestral gods, disembodied and depersonalized, invaded the interstices of the objective world and impregnated the imagination with an interminable variety.[27]

Wilmore goes on to describe the fluidity and fusing between African religious rites and traditions and the slaves' embrace of Christianity. From the Ivory Coast through the Caribbean and throughout most of the African Diaspora, Wilmore explains, African peoples retained a sense of the spirituality they practiced in Africa and a spiritual connection to the land of Africa through their unconscious memory and by remembering of religious rites as best as they could in their new context. Regardless of the depths of oppression that they encountered and lived with, slaves preserved their African rites and religious traditions by fusing them with the Christianity they came to know, and thus established a new frame for Christianity and other religious traditions they practiced.[28]

As Wilmore, Charles H. Long, Vincent Harding, and other historians of religion argue, certain elements of African religious tradition, rites, and rituals were maintained through the era of slavery, and often through the blending of these traditions with more mainstream religions such as Christianity and Islam. This mixing produced new kinds of religion, religious ideas, and religious orientations. Thus, the "spiritual expression"[29] of African Diasporic peoples should be seen as fluid, or hybrid, in that since the beginning of slavery, there have always been multiple forms of religion and spirituality practiced that inform the African and African American experience.

One can best know oneself by diving into the rich culture and complex religious beliefs of one's African past. This may include a belief in the ancestors, an acceptance of the sacredness of the Earth, and a moral imperative to act communally. Rather than using formidable religious categories as a way of organizing African Diasporic religious expression and experience, we do well to find a more fluid, inclusive, and complex paradigm to truly understand the web of religious expression alive in African, African American and Womanist religious thought.

Conclusion

Remembrance of the ancestors has long played a central role in African traditions; and to know oneself, one must know her ancestors as well as her living community. Though womanism is still relatively young, the field has already remembered diverse foremothers of the movement in an effort to honor womanist roots, and appreciate its inheritance. The three hallmarks of third-wave womanism represent the gifts of a new womanist cohort trying to define themselves and already in the process of creating their own legacy. Celebrating global connections and seeking more fluid crossings between academic disciplines, global activism and religious traditions are part of that legacy. Religious hybridity in particular has always been an organic, if sometimes unnoticed, part of African American religious expression and so represents both a return to one's roots and a new self-definition. And it is the creative tension embodied by these moves that may well determine the character of womanism's immediate future.

Epilogue

The Gifts of Alice Walker

Question: *"Mama, why are people so mean?"*
Reply: *"People are broken, babe.*
          Sometimes they don't want to be whole."
Question: *"Why don't people want to be whole?"*
Reply: *"It takes work."*

The womanist mother-daughter conversation above refers to the process of becoming whole. Often referring to a unity between the body, mind, and spirit, wholeness also connotes a deep sense of knowing and being centered in oneself enough to bring wholeness and centeredness to another. In essence, being whole is knowing one's self so well, and accepting oneself so honesty that one reaches a sense of salvation—salvation in the sense spoken about in the Gospel of Mary wherein salvation is understood as a process or journey of knowing the true self and thus, knowing the divine.[1] In relation to the self, wholeness can refer to the full respect, love, and acceptance one has for her/his full humanity and, thus, their divinity.[2] Wholeness in community often refers to a celebrated communal knowledge and wisdom and a sense of togetherness in which all are provided for and no one is hungry, without shelter of adequate resources for their well-being. In Walker's work, this sense of wholeness in community greatly informs her sense of activism. In a way that pushes readers to become activists themselves, Walker writes to encourage others to ask the question, along with her, "How do we as human beings make ourselves whole enough to deserve the respect and love of each other, especially when there is so much bad history, so much fear?"[3] Interrupting the power of fear by breaking the silence that has kept the antidote in black women's and black people's stories hidden, conversations such as the one above have a powerful impact on African American women and their communities. Sharing womanist story and wisdom from which values and virtues can be assembled uncovers avenues for self-love, healing, communal empowerment, and respect for creation that assist in the everyday lives of African American women and their communities.

Unfortunately, it is typically only after being abused by a social system, beaten at the hands of an invited guest, or "wounded in the house of friend"[4] that many African American women realize they have been bamboozled, psychologically maimed, silenced, and sometimes emotionally manipulated and physically harmed. In a confused daze of being tricked and deceived, and in the midst of bleeding, many African American women find their lives and sense of self scattered about and blowing in the wind. As they begin the hard process of putting their lives back together again, piece by piece, moment by moment, memory by memory, African American women can find the courage and strength to break their silences and come to voice. Reaching for wholeness, they begin to share their stories.

A powerful antidote to the crushing oppressions of external and internalized forms of racism, classism, sexism, heterosexism, and homophobia is the repository of story in African American culture and in the lives of black women, which has served as a "healing balm" and a stream of hope that can provide a "way out of no way." In addition to providing survival strategies, creating tools that build sustainable ways of knowing, and living into wholeness, the sharing of womanist story can also uncover how dominant forms of ethics can be helpful or unhelpful while at the same time cultivate ethical systems that do take cultural circumstances of multiple oppressions seriously. Womanist story not only reveals the necessity for womanist themes such as self-love to combat the existence of self-hate, but also provides road maps for living whole and free.

It takes work to recover womanist stories. As many womanist and black feminist scholars have discovered, moving through the depths of survival accounts, slave narratives, and stories told by auntie, mama, and grandmamma, which unleash the insights of women of the past for the sake of women living in the present, is hard work. It not only requires dismantling the age-old structures of discourse, and deconstructing false images, stereotypes, and falsely written histories of black women, but also requires the constructive work of finding broken stories, piecing together shattered histories, and planting epistemologies that center the voices and experiences of black women. These voices, previously silenced in traditional discourses in an attempt to relegate black women, other women of color, and marginalized peoples to the sidelines of knowledge, must be heard, according to black women writers, artists, and scholars.

For womanists, living out of a sense of mutual relationship and interconnectedness discussed above is also done through interaction with the Divine and having ultimate respect for the Earth and each other. This sense of being interconnected presents a basic moral framework that guides the actions, behavior, and decision-making process of African American women and their communities. Offering anything less than practical steps, values, and roadmaps that lead to living in a way that honors this interconnectedness and promote survival and wholeness for African American women is unhelpful. This is because it does not help women to manage and decrease the weight of multiple oppressions nor restore tongues that have been ripped out and unfairly silenced far too long. Both womanists and black feminists would agree that for a people whose family trees cannot always be found by the convenient click of a button and the quick visit to www.familyroots.com, the work of restoring family and community values can aid in the survival and wholeness of an "entire people" and come through the art of uncovering story and experience. As a primary tenet in womanist ethics, uncovering stories is seen as a way of achieving the moral goal of wholeness in the individual and communal lives of African American women.

In this book, I have maintained this tradition of uncovering and used a three-step womanist virtue ethical method designed by Katie Cannon by which to lift up themes in select nonfiction writings by Alice Walker, examine these themes for ethical implications, and glean values and virtues from these implications. I have used this womanist virtue ethical approach to find moral wisdom in the lives and stories of women of African descent so that virtues, values, and ethical systems can be made available for women living in the present day.

Gifts of Virtue; Gifts of Alice

Alice Walker's contributions to womanist ethics are multidimensional. As this book shows, Walker's nonfiction work, ethic, and sense of

Earth justice are some of the elements of her thought that broaden the scope of womanist ethics. In addition, Walker's method of uncovering black women's stories is a model for womanist ethicists who also share a commitment to uncovering black women's stories.

Walker's purpose for uncovering black women's stories is to provide black people with a sense of empowerment and to stress the importance of black women's insights as valued knowledge and wisdom within the wider discourse of literature. Similar to the way in which Patricia Hill Collins' black feminist method operates in the social sciences, and comparable to the way womanist theology and ethics centers black women's experiences for theological reflection, Walker's emphasizes black women's stories, as a way of showing that black women are also fully human and argues that their stories and experiences be treated equally important in the larger discourses of literature and history.

Adopting the first step of the black feminist method, I began this work with a biographical sketch of Alice Walker's life story. True to black feminist and womanist form, I paid attention to Walker's life experience as a way of presenting her life of activism as an important source for womanist ethics. Walker's involvement with the civil rights movement, her adoption of a nonviolent philosophy and commitment to feminism color her lenses and construct her worldview.

Examination of Walker's ethical writings reveals a six-step method for gleaning values from resources authored and stories told by women of African descent. Perhaps the most significant contribution of this book is the analysis of this six-step method that Walker uses when approaching ethical issues, which centers the stories of black women first by recording their own voices and experiences. The first step leads to the second in that by uncovering black women's stories one also validates them as important sources. This second step authorizes black women's stories for ethical inquiry and reflection. The third step examines black women's stories and experiences for values. An illustration of this step is discussed in chapter 4, as I use Alice Walker's writings detailing her mother's story and examine it for values. The values that we unearthed in this analysis include good community, mutuality in relationship (communal interdependence), communal sufficiency, being resourceful, in spite of oppression, self-reliance and letting go for the sake of survival. In step four, the values uncovered are connected to wisdom and this is used to promote justice. Steps five and six are praxis oriented and illustrate the importance of acting upon the wisdom and knowledge gleaned from black women and allowing the sense of empowerment gained from their stories to push people to fight for justice.

Alice Walker: Contributions

If third-wave womanism invites us to extend beyond old categories and limits, how might coming back to Alice Walker—returning to the source—inspire such growth? How does Walker's own journey toward wholeness offer both a model and direction for expanding womanist religious discourse?

A remarkable shift in Walker's writing occurs in the mid- to -late 1980s. Walker had given birth to the womanist definition, firmly established herself and other writers, including Zora Neale Hurston, as primary voices in the black women's literary tradition, and powerfully introduced the womanist idea into fields like psychology, literature, and religion. Then her writing transforms opening up into a new direction away from a sole focus on black women and the womanist consciousness to an emphasis on love for all humanity and the Earth. Just as the new womanist consciousness hits the stage of the academy and womanist parameters are being set to measure what is and is not womanist discourse, Alice Walker appears to move on, setting her sights on the next stage, giving birth to a new voice in her writing, and accepting the challenge to face new social and environmental issues head on that risked being excluded from the womanist-only lens. Taking a risk to change, Walker shifts from the womanist focus found in *In Search of Our Mothers' Gardens* and *The Color Purple* to address issues that seem to have evaded the Black Power movement, among them a commitment to and sacred practice of honoring Mother Earth.

In her book of poetry, *Horses Make the Landscape More Beautiful*, it is easy to see her attempt to grapple with her emerging Native American and Earth-spirituality as well as her own triracial identity. In a poem-dedication to the book, she envisions her African American, Native American, and White ancestors—living together in the spirit realm and inside of her—and begins to address the many tensions that the memories of their human lives embody inside her body. She notes, for example, that all she knows about her great-great-grandfather on her father's side is that he may have been Anglo-Irish and that he raped a girl eleven years old, who was a slave and also her great-great-grandmother. If there is more on this girl's story,

Walker does not say; however, she does tell the reader of her great-grandmother on her mother's side, who is of Cherokee and African American heritage. The rich merging of these two identities on her mother's side, as well as how the historical significance of slavery, rape, racial injustice, and violence against girls and women reveals itself in the stories from her father's side, is laid out ever so softly in her poetry. As she takes courage to connect her triracial identities she pricks the human mind to take account of U.S. history and humans of all cultures to take responsibility for the violent manifestations of oppression.

As Walker invites the reader in her essay "In the Closet of the Soul,"[5] to imagine with her a spiritual realm wherein all these ancestors wrestle with the reality and complexity of their human lives, she opens the door to a conversation about the interconnectedness of humanity, even beyond racial categories. Still holding on to a part of her womanist identity in that she models the womanist tenets of knowing yourself, loving yourself regardless, and coming fully to voice in order to resist oppression and fight for communal and personal wholeness, Alice Walker models the importance of intersectional analysis when engaging the human condition.

Walker's spiritual cosmology is apparent also in her latter essays, and many of the essays included in the second volume of her nonfiction work, *Living by the Word*. According to scholar Karla Simcikova, this book reveals a shift in Walker's thought as she engages a new Native American consciousness, accepts her own heritage, and adopts a spiritual cosmology based upon the sacredness of the Earth. Instead of the racially segregated forms of heaven and hell that she was introduced to as a child, having been taught in the tradition of her parents' Christianity, Walker's writings suggest a cosmology wherein ancestors are connected to living humans, humans are connected to animals, and plant forms are instruments that create a delicate balance in the universe.

Her essay "Everything Is a Human Being"[6] suggests that a cosmology emerging out of Native American spirituality and reflective of African religious tradition be regarded as central for living into an ethical imperative for Earth justice. Having moved from her analysis of her triracial self, Walker's writings suggest a move away from the more rigid categories of spirit prevalent in the Christianity of her youth and toward an inner motion of Spirit power evident in black women's stories, present in the essence of humanity and grounded in the core of the Earth.

It is not until Walker's essay "The Only Reason You Want to Go to Heaven..." is published in 1995 that we gain a wider sense and knowledge of her cosmology and spiritual beliefs. Though her Native American consciousness is mentioned in essays, such as "My Big Brother Bill,"[7] it is in this paramount essay, subtitled "Clear Seeing Inherited Religion and Reclaiming the Pagan Self," that we are given a grander notion of Alice Walker's spirituality and insight on how her fluid path, which includes Christianity, Native American spirituality, Buddhism, and Pagan or Earth religion, presents a model and base from which to argue the importance of being religiously inclusive, and open to the study of a variety of religious traditions alive in womanist spirituality.

Alice Walker is a unique model for womanist religious thought because of her passion for and deep engagement with religion and spirituality. She, like Zora Neale Hurston, does not claim to be a theologian, a womanist ethicist, or religious scholar. Yet her courage and freedom not only to investigate but also to practice and embody various spiritual paths to see if they fit and empower her offer healthy choices for other African-descended women and peoples of color. Walker models for us the agency to see divinity in forms that empower us, and embrace the courage necessary to transform religious perspectives and doctrines that limit women's roles and powers in faith communities, simply based upon their gender, class, color, or sexual orientation.

Walker chooses her religion based on how life affirming, woman affirming, holistic, communally embracing, and Earth honoring it is. She seems to ask whether the religious tradition or spiritual path leads to reverencing a God who loves and honors you as much as you love and honor God. This kind of agency to engage the very divinity of God as the self and in the self is extremely empowering for womanist religious thought.

Walker does not name herself solely a Christian, but rather acknowledges the influence of this path upon her childhood. Until recently this charge has been one reason womanist scholars may have limited their study of her as a model for womanist religious exploration. However, as this work has shown, we may prove unwise to overlook her ability to raise important theological questions, transform religious categories, and pose alternative spiritual pathways that give birth to new theologies and value systems helpful in building a womanist sense of community. For the third wave of womanist religious thought, Alice Walker is central, not only because she has provided the definition of the word "womanist" as it is expressed in the North American context, but also because her life, activism, and commitments have pushed her past original womanist walls parameters in order to keep the movement growing.

At its core, third-wave womanist approaches are responses to the call for womanist religious thought to expand and make room for her children. One of the hallmarks of third-wave womanism is to emphasize the interreligious landscape of womanist religious thought by acknowledging the various religious traditions and spiritual practices studied, embraced, and even simultaneously practiced by womanist scholars, practitioners, and activists. As mentioned the work of many scholars—including Emilie Townes, Dianne Stewart, Tracy Hucks, Linda Thomas, Carol Dufrene, Debra Mubashshir Majeed, and many others—has added significantly to the growth of womanist study by engaging interreligious and often multireligious dialogue. The question of how womanist tenets, tasks, and values can be reflected in a variety of religious and spiritual practices is an important one to continue asking as womanists construct theologies that are ultimately embracing of and empowering for women and liberating for their communities. Walker's own fluid spirituality as well as her nonfiction essays engaging Native American spiritual traditions, Buddhism, Goddess traditions, Earth religions, and the character and life of Jesus are vital resources for reshaping the field and making it more accessible.

Accessibility to women's knowledge and understanding the development of women's epistemologies is also a primary concern for Walker. For her, access to women's stories not only safeguard women from "reinventing the wheel" but also provide strategies of strength and survival for women facing multilayered oppressions such as racism, classism, sexism, homophobia, and environmental racism. Her work on establishing global links is made most evident in her nonfiction book *Warrior Marks: Female Genital Mutilation and the Sexual Blinding of Women* authored with Pratibha Parmar in an effort to raise awareness about female genital mutilation (FGM). Here she uncovers the layered forms of oppression that result in the acceptance and ritualized practice of cutting away a woman's clitoris, a primary sexual organ, as a rite of passage into womanhood. From a Western perspective, the practice of FGM is considered to be in keeping with a balance and order in the patriarchal system and an attempt to defeminize the woman so as not to upset the male hierarchy. The approach that Walker takes in this book is heroic, not only because of her model of womanist activism but also because of her connection with and ability to build connection with women from across the African Diaspora who are both practitioners and resisters of FGM. As a second hallmark of third-wave womanism, the reconnection of the global links already present in womanist religious thought finds affirmation in the model of Alice Walker.

Studying the method of research, study, and writing that Walker uses throughout her career is also instructive for womanist religious thought. She does not simply engage the methods and approaches of the literary tradition but rather draws heavily upon the methods used by mentors such as Zora Neale Hurston, an anthropologist, to reach the deeper modes of African American life and womanist consciousness. An activist, deeply informed by the work of the civil rights movement and the philosophy and courage of Dr. Martin Luther King Jr., Walker's method is interdisciplinary in that she writes into the public arena. She is a public voice, a cultural critic for the times and issues of the day. Her activism informs her writing. As evidenced in many of her articles included in her third volume of nonfiction work, *Anything We Love Can Be Saved: A Writer's Activism*, Walker's literary method and at times journalist style are only some of the disciplinary methods that she draws upon. She combines these methods with the practical realities of the present day and the womanist wisdom that emerges from her mother, her Southern roots, and San Francisco's open-spirited community and inclusive way of being in the world.

Conclusion

Taking account of the powerful model of spiritual fluidity that Alice Walker embodies, it is clear that part of Walker's contribution to womanist religious thought is expanding the discourse to become more inclusive of religious traditions and spiritual practices beyond Christianity. However, the challenge of engaging Walker does not stop there. *Anything We Love Can Be Saved* appears as a moral cry. Published in 1995, the book leads with an essay critiquing the sexist doctrines of Christianity, includes other writings about the patriarchy practiced in Rastafarianism, and upholds that the woman-affirming, Earth-honoring traditions are religious orientations worth exploring for African-descended women seeking wholeness. However, also knowing the ways in which particular womanist parameters, in womanist theology and ethics, have limited the approaches used in scholarship, and thus, constrained certain critical engagement of deeper theological questions, the study of Walker's writings prompts an important question: ought all that is womanist be saved? We have come to a point in the life of womanist religious discourse where methods and points of analysis have been constructed. However, self-reflection on how the same oppressions that womanists resist may in fact be mutating and taking root within the circle is also necessary. Ought everything in womanist religious thought be saved? Who has womanist religious thought left out on the way toward establishing itself as an academic discourse and in attempts to give birth to practical theologies that are woman affirming and accepted in faith communities? Unfortunately, our success has not come without cost. For there are countless women of African descent whose names do not appear on the womanist role and whose scholarship is considered too risky to publish in collected "womanist" anthologies.

For third-wave womanists, the question is no longer simply how to create spaces for womanist discourse to take place. This course has been run, and we are grateful for this work. Now, we are charged with the question, what really must be saved? What do we love deep enough and long enough to hold on to, and what exclusive, religious-oriented categories are simply too limiting and need to be let go? Sometimes no matter how much we love something, we have to let go. For the sake of wholeness, sometimes not everything is worth saving.

Homophobia is not worth saving. Internalized sexism hidden under a womanist cloak is not worth saving. Intracommunal forms of violence and internalized racism, by which certain skin tones establish a hierarchy above others, are not worth saving. Religious prejudices, resulting in skewed approaches, are not worth being saved. The practice of ignoring classism as an essential category worthy of womanist interrogation both within and outside of womanist circles is not worthy of being saved. Disregarding the Earth and moves toward Earth justice simply because it has been historically marked "a white people's issue" is not a position worth being saved. In fact, womanist religious thought, and third-wave womanist approaches more specifically, ought to take seriously the challenges of facing these issues head on. We begin to do so by honoring each other, by doing our work well, by investing in the tradition of womanist religious thought, and by releasing our own agendas to gain deeper insight from the perspective of another. We commit to being agents of change and transformation in a variety of circles around the globe.

Womanist religious thought is changing. We can no longer hold on to the old categories that decide who is in and who is out. If we silence each others' voices, we will silence ourselves. Make room for your children, womanist religious thought, for there are children who are yet being born, and there are children who are already here. They deserve an Earth, a path full of womanist wisdom and trust, and models worth following.

Notes

Introduction

1. Katie G. Cannon, "The Emergence of Black Feminist Consciousness," in *Feminist Interpretation of the Bible*, ed. Letty M. Russell (Louisville, KY: Westminster Press, 1985); Renita J. Weems, *Just a Sister Away: Understanding the Timeless Connection between Women of Today and Women in the Bible* (West Bloomfield, M: Walk Worthy Press, 1988); Jacquelyn Grant, *White Women's Christ and Black Women's Jesus: Feminist Christology and Womanist Response* (Atlanta: Scholars Press, 1989); and Delores S. Williams, *Sisters in the Wilderness: The Challenge of Womanist God-Talk* (New York: Orbis Books, 1993).

2. This date marks the publication of Katie G. Cannon's essay, "The Emergence of Black Feminist Consciousness" first published in Letty M. Russell, ed., *Feminist Interpretation of the Bible* (Louisville, KY: Westminster Press, 1985), 30–40.

3. Grant, *White Women's Christ and Black Women's Jesus*, 209.

4. For more on first-wave womanist perspectives on Christian categories, including sacrifice, servanthood, and unmerited suffering, see Williams, *Sisters in the Wilderness*; Grant, *White Women's Christ and Black Women's Jesus*; and Weems, *Just a Sister Away*.

5. In addition to these fields, womanism critically engages a variety of disciplines and theological perspectives by helping to expose ways in which racist-classist-sexist-heterosexist and other oppressive norms may operate within the approaches, methods, and studies of various perspectives within religion.

6. For more information on the argument of this sort, see Katie G. Cannon, *Black Womanist Ethics* (Atlanta: Scholars Press, 1988).

7. Contrary to the attitudes of some white feminists who saw themselves as "separatists" and noninclusive of men, Walker's term "womanist" suggests that including black men in the movement of affirming black women is essential. Walker's inclusion of black men in her womanist vision can be seen in her description of a classroom setting in which she was teaching feminist aesthetics, recorded in her essay "Breaking Chains and Encouraging Life," in her book *In Search of Our Mothers' Gardens: Womanist Prose* (New York: Harcourt Brace Jovanovich, 1983), 278–289:

    > A white woman says: "I would love to work with black and third-world women, but I'm a separatist."

"A What?"

"Well, black and third-world women always seem connected to some man. Since I'm a separatist, this means I can't work with them. What do you suggest I do?"

"Personally, I'm not giving up Stevie Wonder and John Lennon, no matter what,' I reply, 'but you should do whatever you want to do, which obviously is not to work with black and third-world women."

8. Alice Walker, "Coming Apart," in Take Back the Night, ed. Laura Lederer (New York: Harper Perennial, 1980). It should also be noted that Walker provides further explication of the term in her essay "Gifts of Power: The Writings of Rebecca Jackson," originally published as part of the collection of nonfiction essays In Search of Our Mothers' Gardens.

9. Walker, In Search of Our Mothers' Gardens, xi–xii.

10. Barbara Smith, Toward a Black Feminist Criticism (New York: Crossing Press, 1977); Angela Davis, Women, Race and Class (New York: Random House, 1983); Paula Giddings, When and Where I Enter...The Impact of Black Women on Race and Sex in America (New York: William Morrow, 1984); Gloria Wade-Gayles, No Crystal Stair: Visions of Race and Sex in Black Women's Fiction (New York: Pilgrim Press, 1984); bell hooks, Ain't I a Woman? Black Women and Feminism (Boston: South End Press, 1981); and All the Women Are White, and All the Blacks Are Men, but Some of Us Are Brave, ed. Gloria Hull, Patricia Scott, and Barbara Smith (New York: McGraw-Hill, 1978).

11. Cheryl J. Sanders, Katie G. Cannon, Emilie M. Townes, M. Shawn Copeland, bell hooks, and Cheryl Townsend Gilkes, eds., "Roundtable Discussion: Christian Ethics and Theology in Womanist Perspective," Journal of Feminist Studies in Religion (1989): 83–112.

12. Ibid., 92.

13. Ibid., 87.

14. Namely, Katie G. Cannon, Emilie M. Townes, M. Shawn Copeland, bell hooks, Cheryl Townsend Gilkes.

15. Sanders et al, "Roundtable Discussion," 83–112.

16. Ibid., 85.

17. Alice Walker, Moved to Speak interview by Scott Winn on November 15, 2000, found on http://www.realchangenews.org/2000/2000_11_15/features/walker_moved_to.html

18. Others have labeled Walker a black theological philosopher within the school of academic black theology. See Fredrick L. Ware, Methodologies of Black Theology (Cleveland: Pilgrim Press, 2002). Scholar Anthony B. Pinn also refers to Walker as a humanist in his work Noise and Spirit: The Religious and Spiritual Sensibilities of Rap Music (New York: New York University Press, 2003). Walker, however, is a self-proclaimed pagan. See the preface of The Color Purple, 10th Anniversary Edition (New York: Harcourt Brace Jovanovich, 1992), xi.

19. Ibid.

20. In her essay "The Only Reason You Want to Get to Heaven...," in *Anything We Love Can Be Saved* (New York: Ballantine Books, 1997), 25, Walker explains Jesus' role in her theology: "I further maintain that the Jesus most of us have been brought up to adore must be expanded to include the 'wizard' and the dancer and that when this is done, it becomes clear that he coexists quite easily with pagan indigenous peoples."

21. It is interesting to note the role of patriarchy and hierarchy that are also established in Christian theological thought and whether the influence of these structures within womanism has influenced womanists' narrow selection of religious dialogue partners. In essence, is it patriarchy within womanism that limits womanists from talking to black women in other religious traditions?

22. This quote was taken from an audio recording of M. Shawn Copeland's response to a question regarding Walker's paganism at the "Songs We Thought We Knew": A Conference Celebrating the Work and Thought of Delores S. Williams and the Future of Womanist Theology, April 30, 2004 at Union Theological Seminary in New York City.

23. For example, Stephanie Y. Mitchem, *Introducing Womanist Theology* (Maryknoll, NY: Orbis Books, 2002) is an important contribution but refers only to Walker's definition of "womanist" and the book *In Search of Our Mothers' Gardens* as it relates to its relevance to the state of womanist theology and ethics. Delores S. Williams, *Sisters in the Wilderness*, also references Walker's definition and highlights *The Color Purple* as an important literary source of womanist theology but does not reference Walker's own nonfiction work. On the other hand, Katie G. Cannon's reference to *I Love Myself When I Am Laughing...And Then Again When I Am Looking Mean and Impressive: A Zora Neale Hurston Reader* (Old Westbury, NY: Feminist Press, 1979) and select essays in *In Search of Our Mothers' Gardens* are recorded in *Black Womanist Ethics*. Her book *Katie's Canon: Womanism and the Soul of the Black Community* (New York: Continuum, 1996) also refers to Walker's nonfiction essays.

24. Sanders et al, "Roundtable Discussion," 85.

25. Walker, *In Search of Our Mothers' Gardens*, 71–82.

26. See Emilie M. Townes's reference to Walker's womanist definition and *The Color Purple* in *In a Blaze of Glory: Womanist Spirituality As Social Witness* (Nashville: Abingdon Press, 1995), 68–88; Delores S. Williams's reference to *The Color Purple* in *Sisters in the Wilderness*, 52–56; and M. Shawn Copeland's reference to *The Third Life of Grange Copeland* during a womanist panel-audience dialogue at the womanist conference given in celebration of the work and thought of Williams and the future of womanist theology, Union Theological Seminary, April 30, 2004.

27. See Cannon's *Black Womanist Ethics* and *Katie's Canon: Womanism and the Soul of the Black Community*.

28. Marcia Y. Riggs, *Awake, Arise & Act: A Womanist Call for Black Liberation* (Cleveland: Pilgrim Press, 1994), 2.

29. Ibid., 2.

1   "A Womanist Story": Alice Walker's Moral Biography

1. Willie Fred, born January 10, 1930; Mamie Lee, born February 15, 1932; William Henry, born March 23, 1943 (died July 1, 1996), James Thomas, born November 21, 1935 (died February 10, 2002); Annie Ruth, born October 31, 1937; Robert Louis, born November 23, 1940; Curtis Ulysses, born July 5, 1942; and Alice Malsenior, born February 9, 1944.
2. Alice Walker, "Choice: A Tribute to Dr. Martin Luther King Jr.," in *In Search of Our Mothers' Gardens: Womanist Prose* (New York: Harcourt Brace Jovanovich, 1983), 142.
3. Alice Walker, "In Search of Our Mothers' Gardens," in *In Search of Our Mothers' Gardens*, 231–243.
4. Evelyn C. White, *Alice Walker: A Life* (New York: W. W. Norton, 2004), 12.
5. Walker, "Choice: A Tribute," 143.
6. Alice Walker, "The Only Reason You Want to Go to Heaven Is That You Have Been Driven Out of Your Mind (Off Your Land and Out of Your Lover's Arms) Clear Seeing Inherited Religion and Reclaiming the Pagan Self," in *Anything We Love Can Be Saved: A Writer's Activism* (New York: Ballantine Books, 1997), 3–27.
7. Walker, "Choice: A Tribute," 143.
8. No birth date or day of decease is given for Albert Walker. For the genealogy of Alice Walker's family, consult White, *Alice Walker*.
9. Ibid., 18.
10. Ibid.
11. For more on the cross movements between Alice Walker's family and her fiction, see White's *Alice Walker*.
12. Ibid., 19.
13. Alice Walker, "Father," in *Living by the Word* (New York: Harcourt Brace Jovanovich, 1988), 14.
14. Interview with Bill Walker referenced in White, *Alice Walker*, 21.
15. Interviews with Annie Ruth Hood Walker in White, *Alice Walker*, 11.
16. Ibid., 13.
17. Even though Alice did not grow up knowing her eldest brother, Willie Fred, he would come to have a significant role in her life and work. She writes about this in "Brothers and Sisters" in *In Search of Our Mothers' Gardens*, 326–331. Here Walker tells the story about how she became reacquainted with her brother at her father's funeral. "I watched my sister cry over my father until she blacked out from grief. I saw my brothers sobbing, reminding each other of what a great father he had been. My oldest brother and I did not shed a tear between us. When I left my father's grave he came up and introduced himself. 'You don't ever have to walk alone,' he said, and put his arms around me. One out of five ain't too bad, I thought, snuggling up" (330).
18. Alice Walker, "The Black Writer and the Southern Experience," in *In Search of Our Mothers' Gardens*, 17.

19. Alice Walker, "Sent by Earth: A Message from the Grandmother Spirit after the Attacks on the World Trade Center and Pentagon," The Open Media Pamphlet Series (New York: Severn Stories Press, 2001), 9–10.
20. White, *Alice Walker*, 26.
21. Walker, "Father," 10.
22. Alice Walker, *Revolutionary Petunias & Other Poems* (New York: Harcourt Brace Jovanovich, 1973).
23. Further reflections on Alice's birth can be found in her lecture to the "Midwives Alliance of North America" in 2001, held just a few days after the attack on the World Trade Center in New York and the Pentagon in Washington, DC. In the published essay, entitled "Sent by Earth: A Message from the Grandmother Spirit after the Attacks on the World Trade Center and Pentagon," Alice tells her birth story. White, *Alice Walker*, 13.
24. Ibid., 15.
25. Ibid., 14.
26. Ibid., 15.
27. Ibid., 14.
28. Ibid., 15.
29. Walker, "Father," 9–17.
30. Ibid., 17.
31. Alice Walker, "Beauty: When the Other Dancer Is the Self," in *In Search of Our Mothers' Gardens*, 386–387.
32. Interview with Doris Reid, White, *Alice Walker*, 40.
33. White, *Alice Walker*, 40.
34. Ibid., 40.
35. Alice Walker, e-mail correspondence June 2010.
36. Walker, "Beauty," 386.
37. Ibid., 388–389.
38. Ibid., 389.
39. See Chapter 7 in White, *Alice Walker*.
40. *Walker,* "Beauty," 390.
41. Ibid., 391.
42. Ibid.
43. Ibid., 393.
44. Ibid.
45. For example, self-love is a central concept in *Alice Walker*'s womanist definition.
46. Alice Walker, "The Civil Rights Movement: What Good Was It?" in *In Search f Our Mothers' Gardens*, 123.
47. Ibid., 124.
48. Ibid.
49. Interviews with Porter Sandford III and Bobby "Tug" Baines in White, *Alice Walker*, 53.
50. Alice Walker, *Anything We Love Can Be Saved: A Writer's Activism* (New York: Ballantine, 1997), xxiv.
51. Ibid.

52. For more on her days in Spelman College, see White, *Alice Walker* and the Spelman College Web site www.spelman.edu.
53. Howard Zinn, *You Can't Be Neutral on a Moving Train: A Personal History of Our Times* (Boston: Beacon Press, 1994), 44.
54. White, *Alice Walker*, 69.
55. Ibid., 80.
56. Ibid., 92.
57. Alice Walker, "What Can I Give My Daughters, Who Are Brave?" in *Anything We Love Can Be Saved*, 90.
58. Alice Walker, "The Unglamorous but Worthwhile Duties of the Black Revolutionary Artist, or of the Black Writer Who Simply Works and Writes," in *In Search of Our Mothers' Gardens*, 130.
59. White, *Alice Walker*, 86–87.
60. Ibid., 99.
61. Interview with Annie Ruth Walker, see ibid., 100.
62. Ibid., 101.
63. Interview with Jane Cooper, in ibid., 105.
64. In this book, I do not focus on Walker's poetry but rather her select non-fiction essays. As argued in the introduction of this work, it is important to engage Walker's nonfiction work in an effort to incorporate her own intellectual thought and religious sensibilities into womanist religious talk and academic dialogue. Including Walker's nonfiction voice in womanist scholarship can help shed light on the doing and living out of womanist ethics.
65. White, *Alice Walker*, 110.
66. Ibid., 112.
67. Alice Walker, "From an Interview," in *In Search of Our Mothers' Gardens*, 245–246.
68. White, *Alice Walker*, 116.
69. Walker, "From an Interview," 247.
70. Alice Walker, *Once: Poems* (New York: Harcourt Brace Jovanovich, 1976).
71. Ibid., 249.
72. White, *Alice Walker*, 129.
73. Ibid., 137.
74. Ibid., 136.
75. Ibid., 140.
76. Ibid.
77. Alice Walker, "Recording the Seasons," in *In Search of Mothers' Gardens*, 224.
78. Alice Walker, "One Child of One's Own: A Meaningful Digression within the Work(s)," in *In Search of Our Mothers' Gardens: Womanist Prose* (New York: Harcourt Brace Jovanovich, 1979), 366.
79. Ibid.
80. Alice Walker, "Coretta King: Revisited," in *In Search of Our Mothers' Gardens*, 147.
81. Walker, "One Child of One's Own," 362–363.

82. Ibid., 367–368.
83. Interview with Yakini Kemp, in White, *Alice Walker*, 222.
84. Interview with Mel Leventhal in ibid., 226.
85. Alice Walker, *In Love & Trouble: Stories of Black Women* (New York: Harcourt Brace Jovanovich, 1972). The publication of one of the stories in this latter text, "Roselily," would later open a new path and genre of writing for Alice at *Ms.* magazine in New York.
86. Interview with Mel Leventhal White, *Alice Walker*, 262.
87. Rebecca Walker would later express her feelings about her parents' separation in her book *Black, White, and Jewish* (New York: Riverhead, 2001).
88. Interview with Annie Ruth Walker, in White, *Alice Walker*, 426. Mrs. Minnie Lou Walker died seven years later in 1993.
89. Alice Walker, "Audre's Voice," in *Anything We Love Can Be Saved*, 80.
90. White, *Alice Walker*, 378.
91. For more details on the chronology of Alice Walker's life and publications, see White, *Alice Walker*.
92. Walker introduces this essay in her book, recalling how the money awarded her for winning first place allowed her and her soon-to-be fiancé (Mel Leventhal) to live "magically...for several months" in one room above Washington Park in New York City. See Walker, "The Civil Rights Movement," 119.
93. Alice Walker, "A Talk: Convocation," in *In Search of Our Mothers' Gardens*, 33–41.
94. Considering the importance both these texts hold for the study of womanist religious thought, the insight about "twin-themes" in *In Search of Our Mothers' Gardens* and *The Color Purple* deserves deeper comparative analysis. Certainly this kind of comparative analysis is a theme beyond the scope of this book and is one to which I hope to attend to in the future. The result of this investigation would produce more scholarship, bridging black women's literature and black womanist thought. An entry point for this project might begin with identifying the theme of sexual violence against black women. Examples of this theme in essays by Walker could be compared with themes of sexual violence in Walker's *The Color Purple*.
95. It is important to note that Walker's short story by the same title, "To Hell with Dying," was first published in the 1967 collection *The Best Short Stories by Negro Writers*, edited by Langston Hughes. Hughes was an important figure and mentor to Walker and helped her publish her first work of fiction, "To Hell with Dying." For more information, see White, *Alice Walker*, 119.
96. These themes are addressed in the following essays in *Living by the Word*: "In the Closet of the Soul," 78–92, "Everything Is a Human Being," 139–152, and "Oppressed Hair Puts a Ceiling on the Brain," 69–74.
97. Alice Walker, *By the Light of My Father's Smile* (New York: Random House, 1998).
98. Walker, *Anything We Love Can Be Saved*, xxii.
99. Ibid.
100. Ibid.

2   A Path Set before Us: Womanist Virtue Method

1. Additional information on the tasks of womanist ethics can be found in Marcia Y. Riggs, *Awake, Arise and Act: A Womanist Call for Black Liberation* (Cleveland, OH: Pilgrim Press, 1994).
2. Patricia Hill Collins, *Black Feminist Thought: Knowledge, Consciousness, and the Politics of Empowerment* (Boston: Unwin Hyman, 1990), 202.
3. Cannon, *Black Womanist Ethics* (Atlanta: Scholars Press, 1988), 77.
4. These are only a few among many other tasks and goals of womanist ethics. For more, see the works of such womanist ethicists as Katie G. Cannon, Emilie M. Townes, Marcia Y. Riggs, and Rosetta E. Ross.
5. Though heterosexism is implied to be a form of injustice worthy of examination in the womanist definition coined by Alice Walker in 1983, womanist religious scholars did not immediately pick up on the importance of including this form of oppression in womanist race-class-gender analysis. Thus, as critiques of womanism were launched by scholars such as Renee L. Hill, black feminists Patricia Hill Collins and Traci C. West, and as second, third, and fourth generations of womanist scholars have appeared on the scene, heterosexism has become a central category of analysis for womanist religious thought. See Renee L. Hill, "Who Are We for Each Other?: Sexism, Sexuality and Womanist Theology," in *Black Theology: A Documentary History, 1980–1992*, 2nd ed., ed. James H. Cone and Gayraud S. Wilmore (Maryknoll, NY: Orbis Books, 1993), 345–351; Patricia Hill Collins, "What's in a Name?: Womanism, Black Feminism, and Beyond," *Black Scholars* 26, no. 1 (Winter–Spring 1996): 16; Traci C. West, "Is a Womanist a Black Feminist?" in *Deeper Shades of Purple: Womanism in Religion and Society* (New York: New York University Press, 2006), 291–295. Also, see the work of Kelly Brown Douglas, *Sexuality and the Black Church: A Womanist Perspective* (New York: Orbis Books, 1999), *What's Faith Got to Do with It? Black Bodies/Christian Souls* (New York: Orbis Books, 2005); and Emilie M. Townes, *In a Blaze of Glory: Womanist Spirituality as Social Witness* (Nashville: Abingdon Press, 1995). Other forms of oppression that threaten the well-being and wholeness of black women across the African Diaspora such as environmental injustice have also been added to multilayered womanist analysis.
6. Cannon, *Black Womanist Ethics*, 3.
7. This term is later described by womanist ethicist Emilie M. Townes in her book *In a Blaze of Glory* as the "wisdom found in autobiographies, speeches, novels, poems, sermons, testimonies, song, and oral histories—in their lives" (11). It signals the extensive list of resources, including the arts, that serve as primary sources of knowledge, or epistemologies, for womanist religious thought.
8. Cannon, *Black Womanist Ethics*, 2.
9. It should be noted that from its origins womanist religious thought has given attention to the sometimes shared experiences of racism, class, sexism, heterosexism, and other forms of oppression suffered by other communities of

color and marginalized groups of women. Increasingly, third-wave womanism and the work of several womanist scholars such as Emilie M. Townes,
Stacey Floyd-Thomas, and Linda E. Thomas include the voices of Latina,
Asian, Native American, Aboriginal, and black feminist scholars, and male
scholars who identify as feminist and are influenced by the womanist idea to
resist white supremacy and sexist social structures.

10. It is important to note that Cannon's effort to validate black women's and
black peoples' virtues, values, and ethics is in keeping with Zora Neale
Hurston's anthropological participant-observer method. This profound
methodological connection established a methodological genealogy for
womanist ethics that deserves a more comprehensive response. I am not able
to offer that here but I will note two important conversation partners in
this dialogue for future work. First, in Linda E. Thomas's essay, "Womanist
Theology, Epistemology, and a New Anthropological Paradigm," *Cross
Currents* 48 (Winter 1998–1999): 488–499, she suggests the importance of
operating with a liberation womanist paradigm and using womanist anthropological methods to continue to include African and African American
women's experiences and stories for womanist religious thought. Second,
regarding the close ties between black feminist and womanist approaches,
it is important to note the significance of Patricia Hill Collins's method for
womanist thought. (See especially Chapter 10 of *Black Feminist Thought*,
"Toward an Afrocentric Feminist Epistemology.") Cannon's more specific
ethical methodological steps, including sifting basic experiential themes and
gleaning ethical implications from those themes, are comparable to Collins's
second step of dialogical reflection; and Cannon's third step of constructing
a womanist ethic, often in resistance to or at least different from traditional
forms of ethics, by forming a set of virtues or a womanist virtue ethic can
be compared to Collins's third movement of coming to voice as resistance. It
is also worth noting that while Cannon's experiential step notes the importance of experience recorded in the writings of black women literary artists,
this step also leaves room for readers' reflection upon their own experience
of reading the literature. Whether this can be noted as another step within
the method is yet to be charted.

11. Eve Browning Cole, "Women, Slaves, and 'Love of Toil' in Aristotle's Moral
Philosophy," in *Engendering Origins: Critical Feminist Readings in Plato
and Aristotle* (New York City: State University of New York Press, 1994),
127–144.

12. Examining the context and cultural environment in which ethical decisions
are made is particularly important for womanist virtue ethics because it
provides grounding information for why certain values, such as *community*,
appear repeatedly in the work of black intellectuals and artists from the
nineteenth century through the present. I am referring here to the work of
such writers as Maria Stewart, W. E. B. Dubois, and in the present day Peter
J. Paris, Marcia Y. Riggs, and Emilie M. Townes. More on the context, cultural influences, and the social milieu that Alice Walker was raised in and
the cultural circumstances that inform her writing are discussed in chapters
3 and 4. Womanist virtue ethics also embodies a self-reflective component in

that it continually reexamines the values and sets of virtues previously held within the culture to see if they are still in keeping with and work toward the empowerment of black women and their communities living in present-day realities. For example, Delores S. Williams, premier womanist theologian, lifts the importance of reimagining the category of suffering captured in traditional Christian thought as it relates to the lives and well-beings of black women in her text, *Sisters in the Wilderness: The Challenge of Womanist God-Talk* (New York: Orbis Books, 1995). Here, Williams directly reveals her understanding of the problem of violence in traditional atonement theories, claiming that the cross is a symbol of violence and that the centrality of the cross in black male liberation theology and its association with redemption "supports a structure of domination (surrogacy) in black women's lives" (168). The violence of the cross is manifested not only in the image of the defiled, bloody, and desecrated body of a naked male Jew, Jesus, but also in the symbolism of the cross that constantly argues for the sacredness of surrogacy. According to Williams, this connection between the cross and the coerced and/or voluntary surrogacy roles is especially dangerous for black women who represent surrogates and would have a tendency to compare their surrogacy roles to the role of Jesus as a surrogate. This move to relate to Jesus on "common-surrogacy-ground" would relegate black women to a place of nonliberation. If, for black women, suffering remains a Christian virtue, then the suffering that some black women endure as a result of sexism, even within their own black church congregations, is considered sanctioned, if not holy, suffering. Williams disagrees then with any theology that inherently promotes the suffering of black women, naming it as the sin of defilement. Also, see Delores S. Williams, "A Womanist Perspective on Sin," in *A Troubling in My Soul: Womanist Perspectives on Evil and Suffering* (New York: Orbis Books, 1993), 130–149.

13. Katie G. Cannon, "Womanist Virtue," in *Dictionary of Feminist Theologies*, ed. Letty M. Russell and J. Shannon Clarkson (Louisville, KY: Westminister John Knox Press, 1996), 313.

14. Aristotle, *The Nicomachean Ethics*, ed. Hugh Tredennick (New York: Penguin Group, 2003), 1976.

15. Ibid., 131.

16. Furthermore, Aristotle's discussion on the lack of agency of slaves also would have turned Cannon to think twice about aligning womanist virtue theory too closely with Aristotle himself.

17. Cannon, *Black Womanist Ethics*, 109.

18. Cannon, "Womanist Virtue," 313.

19. Emilie M. Townes, "Womanist Ethics," in *Dictionary of Feminist Theologies*, 91.

20. Ibid.

21. Cannon, *Black Womanist Ethics*, 6.

22. Ibid.

23. The praxis-orientation embedded within womanist religious approaches is somewhat different from dominant theological approaches that focus solely on theory. Womanist approaches include both theory and praxis, particularly

so that it can continue to be relevant to communal audiences beyond the academy. That is to say, womanist thought, unlike some traditional theologies, is bent toward action or committed to practical change and social transformation. This premise is captured by first-generation womanist Delores S. Williams. In her essay "Womanist Theology: Black Women's Voices," in *Weaving the Visions: New Patterns in Feminist Spirituality*, ed. Judith Plaskow and Carol P. Christ (New York: Harper Collins, 1989), she aligns multidialogical intent with theory and action, thus explaining that practical orientation within womanism is expressed as an element within womanist methodology. The practical "bend" of womanism is also expressed in JoAnne Marie Terrell's "10-Point Platform for a Womanist Agenda: (What Womanists Want)," *Union Seminary Quarterly Review* 58 (2004): 9–12. The article references the collaborative work by a group of womanists who gathered to share ideas about the future development of womanism in 2003. In the article, points 2 and 4 signal the praxis-orientation of womanism. "[Point 2] The conscientization of black women particularly and the public generally about the womanist idea as articulated by Alice Walker and as being developed by womanist activists, scholars and ministers, through personal example and public address. [Point 3] The creation of opportunities for dialogue and cooperation between womanist (and proto-womanist) activists, scholars and ministers engaged in struggle for the social, political, economic, intellectual and spiritual empowerment of black women" (9–12).

24. Cannon, *Black Womanist Ethics*, 6.

3   Doing the Work: Building a Womanist Virtue Ethic

1. Emilie M. Townes, *Womanist Ethics and the Cultural Production of Evil* (New York: Palgrave Macmillan, 2006).

2. Emilie M. Townes, "The Womanist Dancing Mind: Speaking to the Expansiveness of Womanist Discourse," in *Deeper Shades of Purple: Womanism in Religion and Society*, ed. Stacey Floyd-Thomas (New York: New York University Press), 246.

3. The reader will recall from the first chapter that both these imperatives are reasons that Walker came up with the term "womanist" in the first place. See Alice Walker, "Coming Apart," in *Take Back the Night*, ed. Laura Lederer (New York: Harper Perennial, 1980) and Alice Walker, "Audre's Voice," in *Anything We Love Can Be Saved: A Writer's Activism* (New York: Ballantine Books, 1997), 79–82. In the latter essay, Walker points out an additional distinction of womanist. Noting a conversation with Audre Lorde, Walker clarifies the meaning of the word: "She [Lorde] had questioned my use of the word 'womanist' in lieu of 'black feminist,' saying that it appeared to be an attempt to disclaim being feminist;...I pointed out to her that it is a necessary act of liberation to name oneself with words that fit; that this was a position her own work celebrated.... We talked until Audre seemed to understand my point about using the word 'womanist': more

room in it for changes, said I, sexual and otherwise. More reflective of black women's culture, especially Southern culture. As a woman of Caribbean heritage, she appreciated this point, I think" (80).

4. Alice Walker, "Choosing to Stay at Home," in *In Search of Our Mothers' Gardens* (New York: Harcourt Brace Jovanovich, 1983), 158–170.

5. Ibid., 161.

6. Readers will note the similarity of Walker's experience to the concept of double-consciousness explicated by W. E. B. Dubois. See W. E. B. Du Bois, *The Souls of Black Folk* (Chicago: A. C. McClurg; Cambridge: Cambridge University Press, John Wilson and Son, 1903; Bartleby.com, 1999. www. bartleby.com/114/. March 1, 2010).

7. Alice Walker, "Beyond the Peacock: The Reconstruction of Flannery O'Connor," in *In Search of Our Mothers' Gardens: Womanist Prose* (New York: Harcourt Brace Jovanovich, 1983), 42–59.

8. Walker, "Beyond the Peacock," 48.

9. For more on the protest writing style, see Emilie M. Townes, *Womanist Justice, Womanist Hope* (Atlanta: Scholars Press, 1993).

10. Alice Walker, "The Black Writer and the Southern Experience," in *In Search of Our Mothers' Gardens*, 21.

11. Peter J. Paris, *The Spirituality of African Peoples: The Search for a Common Moral Discourse* (Minneapolis: Fortress Press, 1995), 130.

12. I refer here to Paulo Freire's concept that the oppressor can lose a level of his/her own humanity by engaging in acts of injustice and unfair treatment of those who are oppressed. See *Pedagogy of the Oppressed* (New York: Seabury Press, 1970).

13. Alice Walker, "The Civil Rights Movement: What Good Was It?" in *In Search of Our Mothers' Gardens*, 122.

14. Walker, "Beyond the Peacock," 42.

15. Ibid., 58.

16. Alice Walker, "Saving the Life that Is Your Own: The Importance of Models in the Artist Life," in *In Search of Our Mother's Gardens*, 12.

17. This example raises a valuable discussion about Hurston's methodological influence on Walker's method and style. This is particularly intriguing when one considers establishing a womanist methodological genealogy linking Hurston to Walker, Cannon's use of Hurston in her womanist ethical analysis, and Hurston's influence on other womanist religious scholars, such as Linda A. Thomas, who use an anthropological method.

18. A colleague of Alice Walker, Toni Morrison, also observes the link between racism and the way in which black history is made in her essay "Site of Memory," in *Inventing the Truth: The Art and Craft of Memoir*, ed. William Zinsser and Russell Baker (Boston: Houghton Mifflin, 1987), 101–124. In the work, Morrison alludes to the racist undertones of how white scholars and historians have often told black history from their own perspective. Reflecting on her own style and method, she writes, "For me—a writer in the last quarter of the twentieth century…a writer who is black and a woman…My job becomes how to rip that veil drawn over 'proceedings too terrible to relate.' The exercise is also critical for any person who is black, or

who belongs to any marginalized category, for, historically, we were seldom invited to participate in the discourse even when we were its topic" (110). Also, see the work of Charles H. Long, *Significations: Signs, Symbols, and Images in the Interpretation of Religion* (Aurora, CO: Davies Group, 1986) for additional crucial insights on the importance of black history being told from the perspective of black people.

19. This term is used by Delores Williams to connote the ways in which black women's stories and experiences are left out or erased from history and theological inquiry in her essay "A Womanist Perspective on Sin," in *A Troubling in My Soul: Womanist Perspectives on Evil and Suffering*, ed. Emilie M. Townes (Maryknoll, NY: Orbis Books, 1993), 147.

20. The reader will note the similar observations made here by black feminist scholar Patricia Hill Collins and womanist scholar Katie G. Cannon regarding the importance of uncovering black women's stories as valid epistemologies.

21. Walker, "A Talk: Convocation 1972," in *In Search of Our Mothers' Gardens*, 36.

22. Ibid.

23. For more on first phase, or first-generation, feminist perspectives, see bell hooks, "Feminism for Everybody: Passionate Politics" (Cambridge, MA: South End Press, 2000).

24. Alice Walker, "The Unglamorous but Worthwhile Duties of the Black Revolutionary Artist, or of the Black Writer Who Simply Works and Writes," in *In Search of Our Mothers' Gardens*, 135.

25. Alice Walker, "Acknowledgements," in *Anything We Love Can Be Saved*, xiv.

26. Further dialogue about Walker's sense of wholeness in conversation with the sense of wholeness described in the work of Emilie M. Townes and Karen Baker-Fletcher deserves additional scholarly attention but spans outside the purview of this project.

27. Alice Walker, "From an Interview," in *In Search of Our Mothers' Gardens*, 250.

28. Alice Walker, "In Search of Our Mothers' Gardens," in *In Search of Our Mothers' Gardens*, 231–243.

29. Walker, "The Black Writer and the Southern Experience," 15–21, and "The Unglamorous but Worthwhile Duties of the Black Revolutionary Artist," 130–138.

30. Walker, "The Black Writer and the Southern Experience," 21.

31. Walker, "The Unglamorous but Worthwhile Duties of the Black Revolutionary Artist," 135.

32. Walker, "A Talk: Convocation 1972," 34.

33. Delores S. Williams, "Sin, Nature and Black Women's Bodies," in *Ecofeminism and the Sacred*, ed. Carol J. Adams (New York: Continuum, 1993), 24–29.

34. Alice Walker, "Heaven Belongs To You: *Warrior Marks* as a Liberation Film," in *Anything We Love Can Be Saved*, 150.

35. Ibid.

36. Walker, "The Civil Rights Movement: What Good Was It?" 123.
37. Ibid., 124.
38. Walker, "The Unglamorous but Worthwhile Duties of the Black Revolutionary Artist," 134.
39. Alice Walker, "'Nobody Was Supposed to Survive': The MOVE Massacre," in *Living by the Word* (New York: Harcourt Brace Jovanovich, 1989), 153–162.
40. Ibid., 155.
41. Ibid.
42. Ibid.
43. Ibid., 159.
44. Ibid., 160.
45. Ibid., 156.
46. In this regard, it is important to note that Alice Walker is not suggesting that Ramona Africa's suffering or survival is redemptive in any way.
47. This is a black cultural colloquium, often quoted as a womanist phrase that has significant religious and spiritual meaning as well.
48. Walker, "Choosing to Stay at Home: Ten Years after the March on Washington," in *In Search of Our Mothers' Gardens,* 162.
49. Walker, "The Civil Rights Movement: What Good Was It?" 124.
50. It is important to note that race, class, gender, and heterosexist analytical categories are not the only categories Walker's definition suggests are important to the black woman's experience. The definition of "womanist" also includes reference to the notion and practice of colorism between black people and attends to the reality of colorism practiced between black people and the wider society. More on colorism is discussed by Babydoll Kennedy, "Quiet As It's Kept: Interrogating the Nexus of Colorism through Use of 'The Bluest Eye'" (paper presented at the annual meeting of the Society of Christian Ethics, Phoenix, Arizona, January 2006).
51. For excellent analysis of this, see Traci C. West, *Disruptive Christian Ethics: When Racism and Women's Lives Matter* (London: Westminster John Knox Press, 2006).
52. Walker, "In the Closet of the Soul," in *Living by the Word,* 79.
53. Ibid., 91.
54. Alice Walker, "This Side of Glory: *The Autobiography of David Hillard and the Story of the Black Panther Party* by David Hillard and Lewis Cole," in *Anything We Love Can Be Saved: A Writer's Activism,* 158.
55. Other writings such as *The Color Purple* also show how violence against women can occur by the hands of women as a result of internalized sexism.
56. Walker, "In the Closet of the Soul," 80.
57. Walker, "Heaven Belongs to You," 149.
58. Alice Walker, "Brothers and Sisters," in *In Search of Our Mothers' Gardens,* 326.
59. Walker makes a point of stressing that her father "expected all of his sons to have sex with women," possibly suggesting that the thought of his sons expressing their sexuality with other men never crossed her father's mind. Considering the historical context and culture of the time, one can only

speculate as to whether Mr. Walker considered notions of black male sexuality that included homosexuality.

60. Walker, "Brothers and Sisters," 327.
61. Ibid., 330.
62. See Alice Walker, "Coming Apart: By Way of Introduction to Lorde, Teish and Gardner," in *Take Back the Night: Women on Pornography*, ed. Laura Lederer (New York: William Morrow, 1980).
63. Alice Walker, "All the Bearded Irises of Life," in *Living by the Word*, 1989), 163–169.
64. Ibid., 166.
65. Alice Walker, "Audre's Voice," in *Anything We Love Can Be Saved: A Writer's Activism* (New York: Ballantine Books, 1997), 79–82.
66. Born out of two schools of thought, black theology and feminist theology, womanist theology and ethics were established to allow black women religious scholars to name themselves and name their own reflections of God and humanity as authoritative. See the introduction for more information.
67. See Cheryl J. Sanders, Katie G. Cannon, Emilie M. Townes, M. Shawn Copeland, bell hooks, and Cheryl Townsend Gilkes, "Roundtable Discussion: Christian Ethics and Theology in Womanist Perspective," *Journal of Feminist Studies in Religion* 5 (Fall 1989): 83–112.
68. Alice Walker, *"Gifts of Power: The Writings of Rebecca Jackson,"* in *In Search of Our Mothers' Gardens*, 81.
69. Ibid., 79–80.

4   Stay on the Path, Walk the Journey: Values to Hold On

1. One example of this is the expository style and language that can be found in Alice Walker, *The Color Purple* (New York: Harcourt Brace Jovanovich, 1982).
2. Alice Walker, "Choosing to Stay at Home," in *In Search of Our Mothers' Gardens: Womanist Prose* (New York: Harcourt Brace Jovanovich, 1983), 158–170.
3. Alice Walker, "Looking for Zora," in *In Search of Our Mothers' Gardens*, 93–116.
4. Alice Walker, dedication to *I Love Myself When I Am Laughing...and Then Again When I Am Looking Mean and Impressive: A Zora Neale Hurston Reader*, ed. Alice Walker (New York: Feminist Press, 1979).
5. Alice Walker, "Zora Neale Hurston: A Cautionary Tale and a Partisan View," in *In Search of Our Mothers' Gardens*, 92.
6. Alice Walker, "The Black Writer and the Southern Experience," in *In Search of Our Mothers' Gardens*, 15–21.
7. Ibid., 16.
8. Alice Walker, "Father," in *Living by the Word: Selected Writings—1973–1987* (New York: Harcourt Brace Jovanovich, 1988), 9–17.

9. Alice Walker, "The Unglamorous but Worthwhile Duties of the Black Revolutionary Artist, or Of the Black Writer Who Simply Works and Writes," in *In Search of Our Mother's Gardens*, 135.

10. Alice Walker, "Everything Is a Human Being," in *Living By the Word*, 147.

11. More on this connection can be seen in my later work on ecowomanism.

12. For more on "interdependent web of existence," see the phrase as recorded in the Unitarian Universalist Church principles at www.uua.org. This allusion to the Web-like relationship between humanity and creation is also discussed by ecological ethicists. See, for example, Larry Rasmussen, *Earth Community, Earth Ethics* (Maryknoll, NY: Orbis, 1998).

13. Though discussion on Walker's ethical imperative for earth justice is limited in this volume, this is a subject of interest for author's future work.

14. Ibid., 16.

15. It is important to note Walker's critique of Christianity in this passage as a religious tradition that was passed onto them by slave owners, but black people transformed it into a life-affirming tradition and set of beliefs that empowered them to survive and thrive.

16. Alice Walker, "The Only Reason You Want to Go to Heaven...," in *Anything We Love Can Be Saved*, 13.

17. Walker, "The Unglamorous but Worthwhile Duties of the Black Revolutionary Artist, or Of the Black Writer Who Simply Works and Writes," in *In Search of Our Mothers' Gardens*, 135.

18. See Walker's account of losing one of her eyes, in part because no white person would stop to help her at her father's request. See "Beauty: When the Other Dancer Is the Self," in *In Search of our Mothers' Gardens*, 384–393.

19. Walker, "Black Writer," 17.

20. Walker, "The Only Reason You Want to Go to Heaven," 24.

21. Ibid., 25.

22. Generosity is an important virtue in womanist ethics and is discussed in chapter 5.

23. For more on virtue theory and the primary moral goal that is reflected in a set of canonical virtues when constructing a virtue ethic, see Peter J. Paris, *Virtues and Values: The African and African American Experience* (Minneapolis: Fortress Press, 2004).

24. Walker, *The Black Writer*, 16.

25. Walker, "Black Writer," 17

26. Ibid., 16.

27. Ibid.

28. Ibid., 16.

29. Walker, "Choosing to Stay at Home," 162.

30. Walker, "Black Writer," 17.

31. In her later essay "This Was Not an Area of Large Plantations: Suffering Too Insignificant for the Majority to See," in *We Are the Ones We Have Been Waiting For* (New York: New Press, 2006), 88–110, she again alludes to this point of focusing on survival, instead of holding onto bitterness and anger. Here, she provides a wisdom approach to help people deal with racism, asking the question, "Suppose someone shot you with an arrow, right

in the heart. Would you spend your time screaming at the archer, or even trying to locate him? Or would you try to pull the arrow out of your heart?" Illustrating the significance of the teachings of Buddhist meditation, Walker explains that fussing at the archer will only keep the arrow lodged in one's heart or, in other words, being angry about racism will not eliminate it but rather, push it further into society as an ill. Instead, Walker suggests finding ways to learn to "free yourself from the pain of being shot, no matter who the archer might be" (103–104).

32. It is important to note that the theme of survival is a central one of womanist thought, established primarily in the work of Delores S. Williams, *Sisters in the Wilderness: The Challenge of Womansit God-Talk* (Maryknoll, NY: Orbis Books, 1993). Theologian Dianne M. Stewart explains Williams's emphasis on survival in "Womanist God-Talk on the Cutting Edge of Theology and Black Religious Studies: Assessing the Contribution of Delores Williams," *Union Seminary Quarterly Review* 58 (2004): 65–83. She writes that Williams's theology of survival "permits an honest evaluation of their [black women's] oppression as well as their strategies for living and affirming their worth and the worth of their communities in spite of racism, sexism, poverty, and violence" (86–87).

33. Walker, introduction to *Anything We Love Can Be Saved*, xxii.

34. Ibid.

35. Walker, "The Only Reason You Want to Go to Heaven," 9–17.

36. Additional reflections of Walker's activism are also found throughout her essays in *In Search of Our Mothers' Gardens*. In essays such as "The Civil Rights Movement: What Good Was It?" and book reviews such as "Nuclear Madness," Walker writes about the necessity of black women, black people, and all people of color to fight and face racial and human inequality and global and earth injustice.

37. Alice Walker, "Nuclear Madness: What You Can Do," in *In Search of Our Mothers' Gardens*, 345.

38. See Peter J. Paris *Virtues and Values: The African and African American Experience* (Minneapolis: Fortress Press, 2004), as well as in this parental volume *The Spirituality of African Peoples: The Search for a Common Moral Discourse* (Minneapolis: Fortress Press, 1995).

5 Take Back Your Life: Virtues to Live By

1. Audre Lorde, "The Transformation of Silence into Language and Action," in *Sister Outsider: Essays and Speeches by Audre Lorde* (Berkeley: Crossing Press, 2007), 41.

2. Alice Walker, *The Same River Twice: Honoring the Difficult* (New York: Scribner, 1996), 170.

3. Alice Walker, "In Search of Our Mothers' Gardens," in *In Search of Our Mothers Gardens: Womanist Prose* (New York: Harcourt Brace Jovanovich), 233.

4. Ibid., 237.

5. See quote by Alice Walker about her mothers' stories, ibid., 240.

6. Peter J. Paris, *The Spirituality of African Peoples: The Search for a Common Moral Discourse* (Minneapolis: Fortress Press, 1995).
7. Inspiration for framework of the following virtues is derived from Peter J. Paris' *The Spirituality of African Peoples: The Search for a Common Moral Discourse* (Minneapolis: Fortress Press, 1995).
8. Alice Walker, "Only Justice Can Stop a Curse," in *In Search of Our Mothers' Gardens: Womanist Prose* (New York: Harcourt Brace Jovanovich, 1983), 338–342.
9. Katie G. Cannon, *Black Womanist Ethics* (Eugene, OR: Wipf and Stock), 126.
10. For additional explaination of body right see, Kate M. Ott, "The Education of Deciding Morals: Adolescents, Sexuality Education, and the U.S. Religious Economy" (PhD diss., Union Theological Seminary in the City of New York, 2005).
11. Alice Walker, "To Be Led by Happiness," in *We Are the Ones We Have Been Waiting for: Inner Light in a Time of Darkness* (New York: New Press), 251.
12. *Summa Theologica*, I.I., in *Basic Writings of Saint Thomas Aquinas*, ed. Anton C. Pegis (New York: Random House, 1945).
13. J. Phillip Wogaman, *Christian Ethics: A Historical Introduction* (Westminister John Knox Press, 1993), 87.
14. For more on this, see the author's reflections on the Gospel of Mary found in "Saving the Womanist Self: Womanist Soteriology and the Gospel of Mary," *Union Seminary Quarterly Review* 58 (October 2004): 177–180.
15. Peter J. Paris e-mail correspondence, February 1, 2010.
16. Cannon, *Black Womanist Ethics*, 144.
17. Emilie M. Townes, *In a Blaze of Glory: Womanist Spirituality as Social Witness* (New York: Abingdon Press, 1995), 87.
18. Paris, *Spirituality of African Peoples*.
19. Townes, *In a Blaze of Glory*, 86.
20. Carolyn Medine e-mail correspondence July 11, 2010

6   Third-Wave Womanism: Expanding Womanist Discourse, Making Room for Our Children

1. Malinda Elizabeth Berry, "Changing the Bulb and Turning on the Light: The Power of Personal Agency in Feminist Work." Paper presented at Transformative Scholarship and Pedagogy Consultation at the annual meeting of the American Academy of Religion. Chicago, IL, November 1, 2008.
2. Ibid., 3.
3. Ibid., 2.
4. Susan Shaw and Janet Lee, *Women's Voices, Feminist Visions: Classic and Contemporary Readings* (New York: McGraw-Hill, 2001), 11–12.
5. See Stacey Floyd-Thomas's allusion to the various understandings of the breakdown of generations in a footnote to her own explanation of womanist

generations in the introduction to *Deeper Shades of Purple: Womanism in Religion and Society* (New York: New York University Press, 2006), 13n7.

6. Cheryl J. Sanders, with responses by Katie G. Cannon, Emilie M. Townes, M. Shawn Copeland, bell hooks, and Cheryl Townsend Gilkes, "Roundtable Discussion: Christian Ethics and Theology in Womanist Perspective," *Journal of Feminist Studies in Religion* (1989): 83–112.

7. Monica Coleman, with responses from Katie G. Cannon, Arisika Rasak, Irene Monroe, Debra Mubashshir Majeed , Lee Miena Sky, Stephanie Mitchem, and Traci C. West, "Roundtable Discussion: Must I Be a Womanist?" *Journal of Feminist Studies in Religion* (2006): 85–134.

8. Floyd-Thomas, "Introduction," *Deeper Shades of Purple.*

9. I also disagree with Floyd-Thomas's intention to separate Alice Walker, and her definition of womanist, from the work, activism, study, and practice (i.e., the movement) of womanism. To do so robs womanist thought, and more particularly womanist religious thought, of the rich resources of Walker's nonfiction work and religious and moral ideas for the sake and doing of womanist ethics specifically and womanist religious thought more broadly. Studying Alice Walker's work reveals new insights and poses new levels of theological inquiry important for the development of the field.

10. Chikwenye Okonjo Ogunyemi, *Africa Wo/Man Palava: The Nigerian Novel by Women* (Chicago: University of Chicago Press, 1996).

11. Ifeoma Okoye, *Men without Ears* (London: Longman, 1984).

12. Clenora Hudson-Weems, *Africana Womanist Literary Theory* (Trenton, NJ: African World Press, 2004), 18.

13. It is important to note Delores S. Williams's almost prophetic call for this kind of dialogue in her essay, "Womanist Theology: Black Women's Voices," in *Black Theology: A Documentary History, Volume 2: 1980–1992,* ed. James H. Cone and Gayraud S. Wilmore (Maryknoll, NY: Orbis Book, 1993), 263–272. In the work, and even as womanist theology is in its infantile stage, Williams calls upon womanist theologians to follow a method informed by "multidialogical intent." She explains that this intent will help all womanist theologians to "advocate and participate in dialogue and action with many diverse social, political, and religious communities concerned about human survival and productive quality of life for the oppressed" (269). This call to have multiple dialogue partners so early in the development of womanist theology sheds additional light on how the third-wave hallmarks of emphasizing the global links in womanist discourse and having interreligious dialogue are in keeping with some of the initial visions for womanist theology and ethics.

14. According to me, this term also refers to womanist theology, ethics, biblical studies, and a host of other disciplines that have been previously mentioned, including sociology, history, and visual culture. North American womanists whose work engages and builds upon the work of several African theologians and other religious thinkers from across the Caribbean and other parts of the African Diaspora include Linda A. Thomas, Dianne Stewart, Traci Hucks, and Carol Dufrene.

15. Mercy Amba Oduyoye, *Introducing African Women's Theology* (Cleveland: Pilgrim Press, 2001).

16. Mercy Amba Oduyoye, *Daughters of Anowa: African Women and Patriarchy* (Maryknoll, NY: Orbis Books, 1995).

17. Rosemary Radford Ruether, *Women Healing Earth: Third World Women on Ecology, Feminism, and Religion* (Maryknoll, NY: Orbis Books, 1996).

18. Isabel Apawo Phiri and Sarojini Nadar, *On Being Church: African Women's Voices and Visions* (Geneva: World Council of Churches, 2005).

19. Wangari Maathai, *The Green Belt Movement: Sharing the Approach and the Experience* (New York: Lantern Books, 2003), and *Unbowed: A Memoir* (New York: Random House, 2006).

20. Rachel E. Harding, *Candomble and Alternative Spaces of Blackness* (Bloomington: Indiana University Press, 2000); Tracey Hucks, "I Smoothed the Way, I Opened Doors Women in the Yoruba-Orisha Tradition of Trinidad," in *Women and Religion in the African Diaspora: Knowledge, Power and Performance*, ed. Ruth Marie Griffith and Barbara Dianne Savage (Baltimore: Johns Hopkins University Press, 2006), 19–36; Dianne Stewart, *Three Eyes for the Journey: African Dimensions of the Jamaican Religious Experience* (New York: Oxford University Press, 2005); Carol B. Duncan, "From 'Force-Ripe' to 'Womanish/ist': Black Girlhood and African Diasporan Feminist Consciousness," in Floyd-Thomas, *Deeper Shades of Purple*, 29–27; Debra Mubashshir Majeed, "Womanism Encounters Islam: A Muslim Scholar Considers the Efficacy of a Method Rooted in the Academy and the Church," in Floyd-Thomas, *Deeper Shades of Purple*, 38–53; Arisika Rasak, "Her Blue Body: A Pagan Reading of Alice Walker's Womanism." Paper presented at the annual meeting of the American Academy of Religion, San Diego, California, November 2007); and Linda A. Thomas, *Under the Canopy: Ritual Process and Spiritual Resilience in South Africa* (Columbia: University of South Carolina Press, 1999).

21. Thomas, *Under the Canopy*. For example, in noting the importance of both western forms of protestant Christianity and forms of African indigenous religion among congregations in a South African context, Thomas writes, "The signs, symbols, and practices used in rituals build a bridge between African religion and western Protestant Christianity. While Christian symbols may seem more dominant, indigenous meaning systems are also present. Cultural signs and symbols of blended African cosmologies are evident." (5)

22. Ibid., 5.

23. Emilie M. Townes, *Womanist Ethics and the Cultural Production of Evil* (New York: Palgrave Macmillan, 2006), 2.

24. Ibid., 5.

25. Jan Willis, "Buddhism and Race: An African American Baptist-Buddhist Perspective," in *Buddhist Women on the Edge: Contemporary Perspectives from the Western Frontier*, ed. Marianne Dress (Berkeley, CA: North Atlantic Books, 1996), 81–91. In this work, Willis describes how two religious systems found within Vajrayana Buddhism and a Baptist form of Christianity inform her religious and ethical worldview.

26. Akasha Hull, *Soul Talk: The New Spirituality of African American Women* (Rochester, VT: Inner Traditions, 2001), 1–2.
27. Gayraud S. Wilmore, *Black Religion and Black Radicalism: An Interpretation of the Religious History of Afro-American People*, 2nd ed. (New York: Orbis Books, 1973), 11.
28. Ibid., 27. Historian Charles H. Long's argument about the significance of the African religious base for the study of African American religion also provides invaluable insights. See Charles H. Long, "Perspective for a Study of Afro-American Religion in the United States," in *Significations: Signs, Symbols, and Images in the Interpretation of Religion* (Aurora, CO: Davies, 1995), 187–198.
29. Wilmore, *Black Religion and Black Radicalism*, 11.

Epilogue: The Gifts of Alice Walker

1. See, Melanie L. Harris, "Saving the Womanist Self: Womanist Soteriology and the Gospel of Mary," *Union Seminary Quarterly Review* 58 (October 2004): 177–180.
2. For more on this concept of full humanity see ibid.
3. Alice Walker, "Follow Me Home," in *Anything We Love Can Be Saved: A Writers' Activism* (New York: Ballantine Books, 1997), 172.
4. Sonia Sanchez, *Wounded in the House of a Friend* (New York: Beacon Press, 1997).
5. Alice Walker, "In the Closet of the Soul," in *Living by the Word* (New York: Harcourt Brace Jovanovich, 1988), 78–92.
6. Alice Walker, "Everything Is a Human Being," in *Living by the Word*, 139–152.
7. Alice Walker, "My Big Brother Bill," in *Living by the Word*, 41–50.

Index

Leventhal, Melvyn, 36–39
liberation, 75–76
Lorde, Audre, 43–44, 85, 109,
   161 n.3

Maathai, Wangari, 133–134
memory, value of, 16–17
Morrison, Toni, 162 n.18
MOVE massacre, 73–75
mutuality in relationship, 95–96

O'Connor, Flannery, 64
Oduyoye, Mercy Amba, 132–133
Ogunyemi, Chikwenye Okonjo,
   129–130

paganism, 8–9, 103, 153 n.20. See
   also Walker, Alice,
   spirituality of
Paris, Peter, 62, 117
patriarchy, 71, 82, 146, 153 n.21
Perot, Rebecca, 86–87
Phillips, Layli, The Womanist
   Reader, 128–129

quiet grace, 56, 116

racism
   black, 73–74
   internalized, 28, 63, 71–72,
      80–81, 110
   intracommunal, 148, 164 n.50
Riggs, Marcia Y., 10

Sanders, Cheryl J., "Roundtable
   Discussion," 4–10, 127
Sarah Lawrence College, 32–33, 65
segregation, 22, 29–30, 37, 61, 91
self-love, 27–28, 43
self-hatred. See internalized racism
self-naming, 3, 84–87, 129, 161 n.3
self-reliance, 57, 98–99
separatism, 3–4, 151 n.7
sexism, 77–86, 160 n.12
   in Africa, 81–82

among black men, 78
   in churches, 2, 50
   and black theology, 2
   defined, 78
   internalized, 10, 78
sexuality, of black women,
   82–86
sharecropping, 21–22, 93–97,
   100–101, 115
Shaw, Susan, 126–127
silence, breaking of, 109–110,
   140–141
silencing, of black women, 78–79,
   83–84, 140
slavery, 80–81, 110
   religion under, 136–137
social protest writing, 62,
   66, 120
southern women writers, 64
Spelman College, 30–32
spirituality, of black women, 112
spiritual wisdom, 118–119
subjugated knowledge,
   51–52
suffering, 53, 57, 160 n.12
surrogacy, 160 n.12
survival, 55, 67–68, 75–76,
   167 n.32. See also letting go
   for the sake of survival

theodicy, 53
theology
   African, 133
   black male, 2, 10, 160 n.12
   dominant, 1–2, 160 n.23
   feminist, 2, 10
   womanist. See womanist
      theo-ethics
Townes, Emilie M., 5, 57, 59, 122,
   134–35

unshouted courage, 56

values, defined, 105
vices, 115–116, 118–123

Alice Walker: Works Cited

Once (1968), 35

Horses Make the Landscape More Beautiful (1986), 143

I Love Myself When I Am Laughing...and Then Again When I Am Looking Mean and Impressive (1979), 91–92

The Color Purple (book, 1982), 7, 18–19, 42–44, 46, 79, 110–111

In Search of Our Mothers' Gardens (1983)

"Beauty: When the Other Dancer Is the Self," 25, 97

"Beyond the Peacock: The Reconstruction of Flannery O'Connor," 61–63

"The Black Writer and the Southern Experience," 69, 100

"Brothers and Sisters," 82–83, 154 n.17

"The Civil Rights Movement: What Good Was It?" 28–29, 63, 72, 76

"Choosing to Stay at Home: Ten Years after the March on Washington," 61, 75, 91, 101

"Coretta King: Revisited," 39

"Gifts of Power: The Writings of Rebecca Jackson," 9, 85–86

"From an Interview," 68

"Nuclear Madness: What You Can Do," 104, 167 n.36

"One Child of One's Own: A Meaningful Digression within the Work(s)," 38

"Only Justice Can Stop a Curse," 115

"Recording the Seasons," 38

"Saving the Life that Is Your Own: The Importance of Models in the Artist's Life," 64–65, 92–93

"In Search of Our Mothers' Gardens," 16–17, 112

"The Unglamorous but Worthwhile Duties of the Black Revolutionary Artist," 32, 69, 70, 72, 94, 96

The Color Purple (film, 1985), 43–45, 78–79, 111–112

Living by the Word (1988)